Readings on Religion as News

Readings
on Religion
as News

edited by Judith M. Buddenbaum and Debra L. Mason

Iowa State University Press /Ames

Judith M. Buddenbaum is a professor in the Department of Journalism and Technical Communication at Colorado State University. Besides teaching journalism, Buddenbaum has been a newspaper religion reporter, a free-lance magazine reporter specializing in religion, and a communication researcher for Lutheran World Federation. Widely published, she is the author of *Reporting News about Religion* (1998).

Debra L. Mason is an associate professor in the Department of Communication at Otterbein College, Ohio, and the executive director of the Religion Newswriters Association. Mason is a former award-winning religion reporter and has researched religion in the media for nearly a decade.

Iowa State University Press
2121 South State Avenue, Ames, Iowa 50014

Orders: 1-800-862-6657
Office: 1-515-292-0140
Fax: 1-515-292-3348
Web site: www.isupress.edu

Authorization to photocopy items for internal or personal use, or the internal or personal use of specific clients, is granted by Iowa State University Press, provided that the base fee of $.10 per copy is paid directly to the Copyright Clearance Center, 222 Rosewood Drive, Danvers, MA 01923. For those organizations that have been granted a photocopy license by CCC, a separate system of payments has been arranged. The fee code for users of the Transactional Reporting Service is 0-8138-2926-7/2000 $.10.

♾ Printed on acid-free paper in the United States of America

First edition, 2000

Library of Congress Cataloging-in-Publication Data

Readings on religion as news/edited by Judith M. Buddenbaum and Debra L. Mason—1st ed.
    p.   cm.
   Includes bibliographical references.
   ISBN 0-8138-2926-7 (alk. paper)
   1. Mass media in religion—United States—Influence. 2. Mass media in religion—United States. 3. Christianity and culture—United States.
I. Buddenbaum, Judith M. II. Mason, Debra L.
BV652.97.U6 R43 1999
070.4'49200973—dc21   99-047158

The last digit is the print number: 9 8 7 6 5 4 3 2 1

Contents

Preface

This book is a labor of love. It is also one born of frustration.

As former religion reporters, we share a long-standing fascination with religion and with its influence on individuals and society as well as deep respect for those journalists who have covered and who now cover news about religion. But as academics, we have found it difficult to help our students see the connections between religion and the media that we believe are important for understanding our culture and reporting on it.

Religious histories of America are plentiful, but few even mention the role of the press in spreading religious ideas through society. Standard journalism histories give short shrift to religion both as a cultural force and as a subject for press coverage. While there are, to be sure, occasional articles in scholarly journals, trade and general circulation publications that address some aspects of the subject, material showing the interplay between religion and news is scattered and hard to find. Therefore, we set out to produce an anthology of news stories that illustrates both the role of religion in shaping public opinion and the role of the media in spreading religious beliefs and opinions through society and in shaping people's opinions about religion.

At first we thought the task would be relatively simple: identify a few episodes and issues when religion and/or religion news coverage clearly made a difference, then find a few stories that would show how newspapers and newsmagazines covered the story. But quickly we found ourselves inundated with examples of times when religion made a difference. Similarly, we found so many interesting and varied examples of news coverage that helped shape public opinion that we very quickly found ourselves facing hard choices about what could be included in this anthology and what would have to be excluded.

To keep the book to a manageable length, we chose to focus on religion in the United States. We also chose to eliminate most examples of religion news that those interested in the subject can obtain rather easily without resorting to anthologies. That means there are no stories primarily about religion abroad: the Middle East, Northern Ireland, or Bosnia, the Pope or the Dalai Lama, for example. Neither are there examples of routine stories from modern religion pages or those that have won Pulitzer Prizes. Citations for prizewinning stories can be found by checking the list of stories at *www.pulitzer.org/archive/;* routine ones can easily be found simply by going to a library and looking through recent issues of newspapers or magazines.

Some other stories were eliminated simply because they were so long that including them would have precluded using several other interesting and useful stories. Initially we had intended to include an appendix of other useful stories, but there were so many that the idea proved unworkable. Instead, we have included references for a few particularly noteworthy ones in the introduction to each chapter.

The resulting collection is, admittedly, somewhat eclectic. We tried for variety in subject matter and writing style. We also sought stories from different regions of the country, from a variety of publications and authors— both those that are well known and those that are not. At the same time, we tried to be mindful of our original purpose.

Taken as a whole, the collection illustrates both continuity and change in religion and in reporting. As such, the collection is designed to meet the need for supplementary material in journalism history and media and society courses, as well as allied courses in American history, American studies and religious studies.

In most cases, we used stories from the publication where they originally appeared, but we have sometimes used a version published in another paper as a way of showing how stories from one region spread through the nation in an era when travel was difficult and journalists had neither the news services nor the communication technologies they now use to cover news from around the nation. To the extent possible, we have also preserved the original typographic features, spelling, grammar and punctuation, adding a "[sic]" or an omitted word only where necessary to make it clear the problem is in the original, not in the reproduction. While the stories from earlier years have historical importance, the chapters devoted to the modern era were designed to show the breadth and range of current concerns. Unlike the stories from earlier years, the more recent ones were selected for their value as examples of good religion reporting and writing. Therefore, these stories lend themselves to use in reporting courses.

Chapters in Part 1 treat the period from the first American newspaper through the early years of the nation, when ideological, even religious, journalism was the norm. Part 2 covers the period from the Penny Press through the end of World War II, when newspapers were privately owned and reflected the views of those owners. Part 3 treats the era when individual ownership began to give way to chain ownership. It covers the years between the end of World War II and the constellation of events in the mid-1970s that mark the birth of renewed concern for religion as news. That era of renewed concern is the subject of chapters in Part 4.

Within each section, chapters are arranged as chronologically as possible, given the overlapping and intertwining nature of the subjects that are their focus. For the most part, stories within chapters are also arranged chronologically, but imposed on that arrangement is some grouping by theme.

Many people helped us select the episodes and issues that form the basis for each chapter; many others helped us find the stories. We thank the religion reporters who shared their work with us and other reporters and colleagues in academia who pointed us to important stories. We also thank the librarians at Colorado State University, the Graham Archives at Wheaton College, Indiana University, Ohio University, Ohio State University, Otterbein College, the University of Colorado and the Westerville Public Library for their help tracking down stories as well as those at other schools who provided materials through interlibrary loan. We also thank the librarians at the *Detroit Free Press* and the *Toledo Blade* for their help.

We gratefully acknowledge the newspapers and magazines that gave us permission to use their stories, an Otterbein College National Endowment for the Humanities faculty development grant to cover copyright costs and additional support from Religion Newswriters Association.

Special thanks go to our assistants Hilary Kimes, Carrie Troup, Brian Batch, Elizabeth Honeycutt, Diane Wootton and William Hayes for countless hours of research work and for typing stories or scanning them into computer-readable files. Most of all, we thank our husbands, Warren Buddenbaum and Jack McManus, for being there for us and for helping us in so many ways.

Introduction

According to the conventional wisdom, Americans were once a highly religious people living together in a nation that was truly "under God." But over time both the people and the country lost their religious moorings as they adopted a secular outlook that is inimical to the well-being of both individuals and the nation. The blame for that change rests partly, if not entirely, with the press, which once supported religion but now treats it as irrelevant at best, a joke at worst.

But the reality is not quite that simple. Certainly over time there have been changes in religion and in the religious climate. There have also been changes in the practice of journalism. But from the Puritans to the Promise Keepers, religious people have left their mark on American culture and they continue to do so. And the press has been there, at every step along the way, spreading religiously inspired beliefs and behaviors throughout the country and policing the boundary between "acceptable" and "unacceptable" forms of religiosity.

During the colonial period, almost all Americans who were religious were Christian. But not all Americans were religious. According to recent research published by Roger Finke and Rodney Stark in their 1992 book, *The Churching of America 1776–1990,* a young woman living in the colonies was more likely to have been sexually active before marriage than to have been a member of a church. Even those who were religious and who tried to live their lives according to the tenets of their faith were not religious in the same way. Although the religious diversity existed primarily within a rather narrow range of Protestantism, disputes were bitter.

Puritan Congregationalists vied for power with the Anglicans with whom they shared an uneasy arrangement of multiple established churches in Massachusetts. They were even more suspicious of the generally less pious Anglicans in the southern colonies. By the eve of the Revolution, southern Anglicans had reason to fear both the Massachusetts Congregationalists and the Baptists who, having been driven from Massachusetts into Rhode Island, were now making such inroads in the south that they were beginning to outnumber members of the established Anglican Church. In Maryland, the only officially Roman Catholic colony, Catholics made up only about 10 percent of the population. As in the other Middle Colonies, the overwhelming majority of residents who belonged to any church belonged to a Protestant one but no denomination had a majority or even a strong plurality. Even in Pennsylvania, the Quaker State, Quakers made up less than 10 percent of the population. There were nearly twice as many Baptists, Episcopalians and Presbyterians.

With so many churches to choose from, diversity was becoming the norm. Although some states continued to have an established religion until well into the 19th century, with so many denominations present, establishments of religion were breaking down even in the religiously most homogeneous regions. With each church fearful lest the others gain too much power, any attempt to establish a religion for the nation as a whole would have thwarted attempts to create one nation from disparate colonies.

Although the First Amendment, with its guarantee that there would be no established church and that everyone would have religious freedom, was adopted for both ideological and practical reasons, whether a nation could exist without a unifying religion to undergird it was, and is, the subject for much debate. But, where many feared, and still fear, that the absence of a unifying religion inevitably leads to a decline in religiosity, the opposite has been true.

Every survey confirms that the United States is the most religious of all western developed nations. Nine out of 10 Americans believe in God; more than half are affiliated with a church and 90 percent of those with a Christian church. Even more consider themselves Christian.

But if religiosity flourishes under the conditions of religious freedom that exist in the United States, religious options have also proliferated. Jews and Muslims each make up at least 3 percent of the population; there are almost as many Hindus and Buddhists. An accurate count for other smaller religions is almost impossible, but their combined membership probably does not exceed 10 percent of the total population. Christians remain the majority.

Today there are at least 100 varieties of Christian religions and well over 1,000 other options. Each religion promotes its own beliefs and its own vision of how people should behave and how society should be ordered. With so many diverse beliefs, no single religion can put its stamp on society the way Puritans were initially able to do in colonial New England. As a result, it is easy for members of every religion to assume the result is evidence that religion has lost its influence.

But religion still leaves its mark. As Alexis de Tocqueville noted when he visited the United States in 1831, the freedom the First Amendment grants to all religions has turned them into voluntary associations that must compete with each other for members and for money. This competition has produced a kind of religious vitality and sense of purpose unknown elsewhere. Freed from government control—and support—religion shapes the manners and mores of society. But to do so, religion, like other kinds of voluntary associations, needs the press. As de Tocqueville also noted, only the press has the ability to plant the same idea simultaneously in thousands of minds.

Needing press coverage and getting it can be a two-edged sword. The news about religion that the media choose to cover spreads those ideas throughout society; the choices teach people which religions and which religiously inspired ideas are important and unimportant, which ones are acceptable and unacceptable. That was as true in colonial times as it is today.

Until well into the 20th century, most newspapers were individually owned and operated to give voice to the particular world views of their printers/editors/owners or backers. Writers often used religious arguments, couched in religious language, to promote proper religion as they understood it and to support other causes that they favored. They also used their papers to attack religions and religiously inspired opinions and behaviors with which they disagreed. People expected each newspaper to have a distinctive viewpoint and to be true to it. Neutrality and objectivity were foreign concepts. Anyone who attempted fair and balanced coverage would have been seen as lacking in conviction and, therefore, as morally suspect.

The resulting coverage often exacerbated culture wars even as it fueled revivals and reforms promoted by those religious options fortunate enough to find a newspaper to promote their causes. The result was generally acceptable to most people so long as the marketplace of ideas was understood as consisting of multiple newspapers and magazines each championing their own views and so long as there were many such competing media circulating within the same city or town.

But with the decline in multiple newspaper towns and the rise of corporate ownership, such views became untenable. In order to attract an audience large enough for it to survive, each publication had to become all things to all people. Religious rhetoric dropped out of popular discourse, partly because religious diversity meant the language was no longer as widely shared as it once was and partly because the language of one tradition would be offensive to another. The result was, first, a fairly neutral kind of stenographic journalism and then the kind of objectivity attempted today.

But in spite of the changes, the result has been remarkably the same regardless of whether each religion or religious viewpoint is covered in a separate publication, each one is covered in the same publication by a separate story relatively free from outside interpretation, or whether multiple perspectives are combined into a single story.

The news media pick up on some religions and their attendant behaviors and viewpoints, spreading them throughout society while virtually ignoring other religions and their concerns. The coverage inevitably has an agenda-setting and socialization effect.

Sometimes the coverage has been, and is, hostile to religion or to a particular religion. However, in general it has, and does, support certain themes that, as Mark Silk points out in his 1995 book, *Unsecular Media: Making News of Religion in America,* support widely shared values that are deeply imbedded in a culture that is, at core, religious.

The more things change, the more they stay the same.

The chapters and stories in this book illustrate continuities in issues, arguments and styles of coverage. The stories show religious influence on American culture. They also provide examples of news coverage that helped shaped the religious climate and opinions about religion.

The beliefs and behaviors that concerned and sometimes divided our colonial forebears fuel public debates today. The religiously inspired arguments used then resurface in current debates over very similar issues. The events of the past have their impact on the present.

The kinds of news colonial printers published in their papers are staples today. If the religious essay is no longer the norm, it has not disappeared. Its traces linger on editorial pages, in magazines and as the inspiration for stories that break free of the inverted pyramid. Individual viewpoints are now more often compressed into single stories, but the viewpoints, and the issues themselves, remain a constant feature of religion news. Voices from the past serve as a cautionary tale, a challenge and an inspiration for students of history and for the journalists who write its first draft.

PART 1

Ideological Journalism in a New Jerusalem

When they landed at Plymouth Rock in 1620, the Pilgrims signed the Mayflower Compact in which they "covenanted together," binding themselves to each other and to God. But their Plymouth Colony was absorbed into the Massachusetts Bay Colony founded by the Puritans. Like the Pilgrims, the Puritans came to the New World primarily for religious freedom. But that was a freedom they were unwilling to share with others. Where the Pilgrims had separated church and state, the Puritans combined them.

For the Puritans, America was to be the "New Jerusalem," a "shining city on the hill." To make it just that, both church and state were to be governed by church members—the "elect"—as God's agents in this world. Making that religio-political system work required an educated clergy and a literate church membership, so the Puritans established schools, including Harvard University. They also established printing presses and founded newspapers.

Harvard's press printed books and tracts; clergy, faculty and students contributed to Boston's newspapers. Printed material from Boston spread Puritan ideas through the colonies. But in spite of their best efforts, the Puritans were unable to convince those living in other colonies to adopt their religious beliefs and powerless to prevent other churches from making inroads into their territory. Still, Puritanism left its mark.

If others could not accept the Puritan form of government or agree to their strict moral code, they did agree that people needed instruction in correct beliefs and protection from influences that might lead them astray. They also readily accepted the Puritan vision of America as a special place. Like William Penn, who described his Pennsylvania colony as a "holy experiment," Americans came to see themselves as creating a society that would be "an example to the nations."

That basic idea was reinforced through sermons, tracts, books and

1

finally through newspapers. Until well into the 19th century those news-papers could more properly be described as "viewspapers." In the early years of the Republic, a few printer/editors opened their pages to people on all sides of a controversy. But that model was generally suspect. From the establishment of the first newspaper in 1690 through the era of the Party Press, the prevailing view was that people should have the courage of their own convictions. Those who published, without comment or con-tradiction, views with which they disagreed were generally seen as moral-ly suspect.

During that period, most papers represented a distinctive viewpoint—first that of the paper's proprietor or his financial backers and then that of a political faction or party. On matters of religion, ideological journalism produced a kind of religious news designed to promote and protect correct beliefs and behaviors according to the standards of the newspaper print-er/editor and his supporters.

The stories reproduced in the chapters in this section show continuity and change in journalistic practices during the years from 1690 through the early 1800s. They also illustrate changing and competing views of what the New Jerusalem should look like.

Chapter 1 includes the press philosophies of early newspapers and some very early examples of news about religion. Chapter 2 covers the attempt by Anglicans to capitalize on controversy over a vaccine for small-pox to break Puritan hegemony in Massachusetts. Although that attempt failed, chapter 3 provides accounts of the first period of religious revival, the Great Awakening, which undermined Puritan power by splitting churches and even families. Turning from primarily religious controver-sies to political ones, chapter 4 includes stories illustrating religious argu-ments for and against the Revolutionary War. Chapter 5 treats religiously inspired arguments that accompanied attempts to define a course for the new nation.

1

Early Press Philosophy and Practice

In Puritan New England, the first newspaper publishers saw their newspapers as fulfilling both informational and religious functions. Those twin functions can be seen in the statements published in the first issue of the first newspaper, Benjamin Harris's *Publick Occurrences Both Forreign and Domestick,* and later ones, including Samuel Kneeland's *New-England Weekly Journal.*

After just one issue, government authorities shut down *Publick Occurrences* because Harris apparently published it without first obtaining the required license. By the time the next newspapers appeared, the requirement for a license had been lifted. Although the subsequent custom of publishing "by authority" also died out after 1721, most early printers were careful not to print anything that would offend the community.

The first newspapers downplayed politics. Active newsgathering was minimal. News consisted primarily of short items reprinted or summarized from other papers that arrived in a city via boat from Europe or stagecoach from other colonies. Those items, as well as simple observations about life in the community, blended together. Headlines and typographic features other than italics were rare. As with Harris's philosophy and the news piece that follows, the beginning of a new item was marked only by indenting for a new paragraph.

The philosophy expressed in Kneeland's paper is unusual because it promises contributions from correspondents who would provide news from surrounding communities. An example of that news is an account of the ordination examination of a new minister. However, in Kneeland's paper, as in most other early papers, news of religion consisted primarily of personal experiences that also served as cautionary tales or of first-person accounts that attributed "remarkable events" to divine pleasure or divine displeasure. Those forms are illustrated by Jeremiah Collier's account of a shipwreck and by the "Confession of a Woman Accused of Murder," to which are appended related items and an example of the record of baptisms Kneeland promised in his first issue.

The prospectus for the Georgia Colony is an unusually long example of the kind of documents that newspapers of the era often reprinted in full. It also provides evidence of existing assumptions about the beneficial effects of life in the New Jerusalem.

Although printer/editors outside Massachusetts were less inclined to express a religious purpose in their paper's prospectus or first issue, they, too, generally avoided publishing material that would be offensive to their community. Believing their papers should provide material that would be uplifting and instructive for moral improvement, they often reprinted tracts or sermons. But not everyone found their efforts laudatory.

At age 25, Ben Franklin wrote his "Apology for Printers" after many in the community complained about an offensive reference to Anglican clergy in an advertisement he had printed. The Apology ends with a fable that Thomas Whitmarsh repeated in his *South-Carolina Gazette* of October 14, 1732, in response to his critics.

In opening his paper to all views, Franklin was more successful than most other colonial printers who tried that approach. But his Apology glosses over occasions when he may well have given offense to the religious community: the satires of religion he published under the name of Silence Dogood (see chapter 2), and a fictional story of a witch trial at Mount Holly, which he may or may not have written, but did publish in the *Pennsylvania Gazette* on October 22, 1730. However, the Apology is remarkable for Franklin's view of publishing, which is more in tune with journalistic practices of today than those of his own era, and for his description of problems that continue to plague journalists who cover religion.

Benjamin Harris: Philosophy and First News

Publick Occurrences Both Forreign and Domestick, September 25, 1690

It is designed, that the Countrey shall be furnished once a month (or if any Glut of Occurrences *happen* oftener*) with an Account of such considerable things as have arrived unto our Notice.*

In order here unto, the Publisher will take what pains he can to obtain a Faithful Relation *of all such things; and will particularly make himself beholden to such Persons in* Boston *whom he knows to have been for their own use the diligent Observers of such matters.*

That which is herein proposed is, First, *That* Memorable Occurrents *of* Divine Providence *may not be neglected or forgotten, as they too often are.* Secondly, *That people everywhere may better understand the Circumstances of Publique Affairs, both abroad and at home: which may not only direct their* Thoughts *at all times, but at some times also to assist their* Business *and* Negotiations.

Thirdly, *That some thing may be done towards the* Curing, *or at least the* Charming *of that* Spirit *of* Lying, *which prevails among us, wherefore nothing shall be entered, but what we have reason to believe is true, repairing to the best fountains for our information. And when there appears any* material mistake *in any thing that is collected, it shall be* corrected *in the next.*

Moreover, *the Publisher of these* Occurences *is willing to engage, that whereas, there are many* False Reports, *maliciously made, and spread among us, if any well minded person will be at the pains to trace any such* false Report, *so far as to find out and Convict the* First Raiser *of it, he will in this Paper (unless just Advice be given to the contrary) expose the Name of such person as* A malicious Raiser of a False Report. *It is supposed that none will dislike this Proposal, but such as intend to be guilty of so villanous a Crime.*

THE Christianized *Indians* in some parts of *Plimouth*, have newly appointed a day of Thanksgiving to God for his mercy in supplying their extream and pinching Necessities under their late want of Corn, and for His giving them now a prospect of a very *Comfortable Harvest*. Their Example may be worth Mentioning.

Samuel Kneeland's Philosophy of News

The New-England Weekly Journal, March 20, 1727

It would be needless to mention here the particular Reasons *for Publishing this Paper; and will be sufficient to say, That the* Design *of it is with Fidelity and Method to Entertain the Public every* Monday *with a Collection of the most Remarkable Occurrences of* Europe, *with a particular Regard from time to time to the present Circumstances of the Publick Affairs, whether of Church or State. And to render this Paper more Acceptable to its* Readers, *immediate care will be taken (and a considerable progress is herein already made) to settle a Correspondence with the most knowing and ingenious Gentlemen in the several noted Towns in this and the Neighbour-Provinces, who may take particular Care seasonably to Collect and send what may be Remarkable in their Town or Towns adjacent worthy of the Public View; whether of Remarkable Judgments, or Singular Mercies, more private or public, Preservations & Deliverances by Sea or Land: together with some other Pieces of History of our own, &c. that may be profitable & entertaining both to the Christian and Historian. It is likewise intended to insert in this Paper a Weekly Account of the Number of Persons* Buried, *&* Baptiz'd, *in the Town of* Boston; *With several other Things that at present can only be thought of, that may be of Service to the Publick; And special care will be taken that nothing contrary thereto shall be inserted.*

Jeremiah Collier's Reflections on a Storm and Shipwreck

The Boston News-Letter, June 5 to 12, 1704

Mr. Jeremiah Collier, writing a Letter to a Person of Equality upon occasion of the late Tempest concludes thus,

We have lately felt a sad Instance of God's Judgments in the terrible Tempest: Terrible beyond any thing in that Kind in Memory, or Record. For not to enlarge on the lamentable Wrecks, and Ruins, were we not almost swept into a Chaos? Did not Nature seem to be in her last Agony, and the World ready to expire? And if we go on still in such Sins of Defyance, may we not be afraid of the Punishment of *Sodom,* and that God should destroy us with *Fire* and *Brimstone.*

What impression this late Calamity has made upon the *Play-house,* we may guess by their Acting *Macbeth* with all its Thunder and Tempest, the same Day: Where at the mention of the *chimnies being blown down (Macbeth, p. 20)* the *Audience* were pleas'd to *Clap,* at an unusual Length of Pleasure and Approbation. And is not the meaning of all this too intelligible? Does it not look as if they had a Mind to out-brave the Judgment? And make us believe the Storm was nothing but an Eruption of *Epicurus's* Atoms, a Spring-Tide of Matter and Motion, and a bland Salley of Chance? This throwing Providence out of the Scheme, is an admirable *Opiate* for the Conscience! And when Recollection is laid asleep, the *Stage* will recover of Course, and go on with their Business effectually.

Thus, Sir, I have laid before you what I have to offer upon this Occasion, and am,

Your most Humble Servant,

December 10.

1703   J.C.

Confession of a Woman Accused of Murder

The New-England Weekly Journal, June 19, 1727

(In our Numb. 10, we mention'd the Execution of a Molatto Woman at *Plymouth* for the Murder of her Child, since which we have receiv'd a Paper which was found in the Prison after her Execution, supposed to have been taken from her own mouth by one who was in Goal with her some time of her Imprisonment, and is here inserted, without the Addition of One Word.)

A Short Account of the Life of *Elizabeth Colson,*
a Molatto Woman, who now must Dye
for the Monstrous Sin of Murdering her Child.

I was born at Weymouth *and my Mother put me out to* Ebenezer Prat, *who was to learn me to read, but I fear they never took that pains they should have done to instruct me, my Mother being School-Mistress was loth I should come to School with other Children, and so I had not that Instruction I wish I had in my Youth. I was carry'd very hardly too by my Mistress, and suffer'd hunger and blows, and at last was tempted to Steal, for which I have reason to lament, for although I stole at first for necessity as I tho't, yet the* Devel *took that Advantage against me, and led me further into Sin, for one Lord's Day the People being gone to Meeting, I broke into a Neighbour's House, and stole some Victuals, and looking for more I saw a piece of Money, which I took, and afterwards telling a Lye, & saying I found it, so was led by one sin to another.*

After-wards I was Sold to Lieut. Reed, *where I had some good Examples set me, but having got a habit of Sin, I still grow worse & worse, and was left to fall into the Sin of Fornication, and after my Time was out with Master* Reed, *I was in great distress what to do with my Child, but carried it from place to place, till I left it at Dighton and ran away from it, and soon fell again to that shameful & Soul destroying Sin of*

Fornication the Second time; and not having the Fear of God before my Eyes, I was justly left of God to this horrid Sin the Third time, that led me together with the Instigation of the Devil, and the wretchedness of my own Heart, to that monstrous Sin for which I must now Dye: And so I have not only brought my Body to dye a shameful Death, but my Soul in danger of Death & Damnation.

O that all People would be Warned to flee from the Sins I have been Guilty of, least they run themselves into more terrible Distresses than they can easily imagine, amongst their ungodly Companions, who will not be able to help them out of their Distresses, when they have left God and God hath left them. I would therefore earnestly intreat all Young People to watch against the beginnings of Sin in themselves, for you know not where you will stop this side Hell if once you allow your selves in Sin, tho' you may think you can: For I remember that when I was Young, I heard of a Woman that Murdered her Child, and I said, I never would do so. *I may say to you as my Mistress did to me,* you do not know what you may be left to. *Therefore, I would intreat all Young People to beware of Stealing, Lying, and especially that shameful Sin of Uncleanness, which hath been the leading Sin to that horrid Sin for which I must Dye. O then take this Advice from a poor Dying Malefactor, who must suffer a Shameful Death as the just demerits of a sinful Life.*

O that all People would take Warning by me, of grieving the Holy spirit of God by sinning against the light of their own Conscience, and of Prophaning the Sabbath Day, and not regarding the Warnings of Christ's faithful Embassadours, but be now advised to take fast hold of Instruction, and let it not go, keep it for it is thy Life: And let them then, that think they stand, take heed lest they fall.

We hear from *Hinghan,* that on Tuesday morning the 9th of this Instant June, was found Dead, the Child of Capt. *Stephen Cushing,* 'tho going to Bed well. As also on the same Day was Scalded in a very remarkable manner the Child of *Daniel Cushing* of *Hingham* aforesaid, which dyed the Night following.

Burials in the Town of BOSTON, *since our last,*

Seven Whites ; One Black

Baptiz'd in the several Churches,

Six.

Extract from the Designs for the Georgia Colony

The South-Carolina Gazette, December 2 to 9, 1732

Christianity will be extended by the Execution of this Design; since the good Discipline established by the Society will reform the Manners of those miserable Objects, who shall be by them subsisted; and the Example of a whole Colony, who shall behave in a just, moral, and religious Manner, will contribute greatly towards the Conversion of the *Indians,* and taking off the Prejudices received from the profligate Lives of such who have scarce any Thing of Christian but the Name.

The Trustees in their general Meetings will consider of the most prudent Methods for effectually establishing a regular Colony; and that it may be done is demonstrable. Under what Difficulties was *Virginia* planted; The Coast and Climate then unknown, the *Indians* numerous, at Enmity with the first Planters,who were forced to fetch all Provisions from *England*; yet it is grown a mighty Province and the Revenue receives 100,000 for Duties with the Goods that they send yearly Home. Within this 50 Years *Pennsylvania* was as much a Forest as *Georgia* is now; and in these few Years, by the wise Occonomy of *William Penn,* and those who assisted him, it now gives Food to 80,000 Inhabitants, and can boast of as fine a City as most in *Europe.*

This new Colony is more likely to succeed than either of the former were, since *Carolina* abounds with Provisions, the Climate is known, and there are Men to instruct in the Seasons Nature of cultivating the Soil. There are but few *Indian* Families within 400 miles, & those in perfect Amity with the *English; Port-Royal,* the station of his Majesty's Ships, is within 30 and *Charlestown,* a great Mart, is within 120 miles. If the Colony is attacked, it may be relieved by Sea from *Port-Royal,* or the *Bahamas*; and the Militia of *South-Carolina* is ready to support it by Land.

For the continuing the Relief which is now given, there will be Lands reserved in the Colony; and the Benefits arising from them is to go to the carrying on of the Trust. So that at the same Time the Money by being laid out preserves the Lives of the poor, and makes a comfortable Provision for those whose Expences are by it defrayed; their Labour in improving their own Lands will make the adjoining reserved Lands valuable, and the Rents of those reserved Lands will be a perpetual Fund for the relieving more poor People. So that instead of laying out the Money upon Lands with the Income to support the People, this is laying out Money upon the Poor, and by relieving those who are now unfortunate, raises a Fund for the perpetual Relief of those who shall be so hereafter.

There is an Occasion now offered for every one to help forward this Design, the smallest Benefaction will be received and applied with the utmost Care; every little will do something, and a great Number of small Benefactions will amount to a sum capable of doing a great deal of Good.

If any Person, moved with the Calamities of the Unfortunate, shall be inclined to contribute towards their Relief, by encouraging this Design, they are desired to pay their Benefactions into the Bank of *England,* on Account of the Trustees for establishing the Colony of *Georgia* in *America,* or else to any of the Trustees, who are as follows, *viz.* The Rt. Hon. the Lord Visc. *Percival,* the Rt. Hon. the Lord *Carpenter,* the Hon. *Edw. Digby,* Esq; *James Oglethorp, George Heathcote, Robert Moor, Robert Hacks, John Larvebe, James Vernon, Thomas Tower, Francis Eyles, William Sloper, William Belitha, Rogers Holland,* Esqrs. The Rev. *Mr. Stephen Hales,* B.D. the Rev. *Mr. John Burton, Richard Bundy, Arthur Bedford, Samuel Smith, Adam Anderson,* and *Thomas Corant,* Gents.

Benjamin Franklin's Apology for Printers

The Pennsylvania Gazette, June 10, 1731

Being frequently censur'd and condemn'd by different Persons for printing Things which they say ought not to be printed, I have sometimes thought it might be necessary to make a standing Apology for my self, and publish it once a Year, to be read upon all Occasions of that Nature. Much Business has hitherto hindered the execution of this Design; but having very lately given extra-ordinary Offence by printing an Advertisement with a certain *N.B.* at the End of it, I find an Apology more particularly requisite at this Juncture, tho' it happens when I have not yet Leisure to write such a thing in the proper Form, and can only in a loose manner throw some Considerations together which should have been the Substance of it.

I request all who are angry with me on the Account of printing things they don't like, calmly to consider these following Particulars

1. That the Opinions of Men are almost as various as their Faces; an Observation general enough to become a common Proverb, *So many Men so many Minds.*

2. That the Business of Printing has chiefly to do with Mens Opinions; most things that are printed tending to promote some, or oppose others.

3. That hence arises the peculiar Unhappiness of that Business, which other Callings are no way liable to; they who follow Printing being scarce able to do any thing in their way of getting a Living, which shall not probably give Offence to some, and perhaps to many; whereas the Smith, the Shoemaker, the Carpenter, or the Man of any other Trade, may work indifferently for People of all Persuasions, without offending any of them: and the Merchant may buy and sell with Jews, Turks, Hereticks, and Infidels of all sorts, and get Money by every one of them, without giving Offence to the most orthodox, of any sort; or suffering the least Censure or Ill-will on the Account from any Man whatever.

4. That it is as unreasonable in any one Man or Set of Men to expect to be pleas'd with every thing that is printed, as to think that nobody ought to be pleas'd but themselves.

5. Printers are educated in the Belief, that when Men differ in Opinion, both Sides ought equally to have the Advantage of being heard by the Publick; and that when Truth and Error have fair Play, the former is always an overmatch for the latter: Hence they chearfully serve all contending Writers that pay them well, without regarding on which side they are of the Question in Dispute.

6. Being thus continually employ'd in serving all Parties, Printers naturally acquire a vast Unconcernedness as to the right or wrong Opinions contain'd in what they print; regarding it only as the Matter of their daily labour: They print things full of Spleen and Animosity, with the utmost Calmness and Indifference, and without the least Ill-will to the Persons reflected on; who nevertheless unjustly think the Printer as much their Enemy as the Author, and join both together in their Resentment.

7. That it is unreasonable to imagine Printers approve of every thing they print, and to censure them on any particular thing accordingly; since in the way of their Business they print such great variety of things opposite and contradictory. It is likewise as unreasonable what some assert, *That Printers ought not to print any Thing but what they approve;* since if all of that Business should make such a Resolution, and abide by it, an End would thereby be put to Free Writing, and the World would afterwards have nothing to read but what happen'd to be the Opinions of Printers.

8. That if all Printers were determin'd not to print any thing till they were sure it would offend no body, there would be very little printed.

9. That if they sometimes print vicious or silly things not worth reading, it may not be because they approve such things themselves, but because the People are so viciously and corruptly educated that good things are not encouraged. I have known a very numerous Impression of *Robin Hood's Songs* go off in this Province at 2*s*. per Book, in less than a Twelvemonth; when a small Quantity of *David's Psalms* (an excellent Version) have lain upon my Hands above twice the Time.

10. That notwithstanding what might be urg'd in behalf of a Man's being allow'd to do in the Way of his Business whatever he is paid for, yet Printers do continually discourage the Printing of great Numbers of bad things, and stifle them in the Birth. I my self have constantly refused to print any thing that might countenance Vice, or promote Immorality; tho' by complying in such Cases with the corrupt Taste of the Majority, I might have got much Money. I have also always refus'd to print such things as might do real Injury to any Person, how much soever I have been solicited, and tempted with Offers of great Pay; and how much soever I have by refusing got the Ill-will of those who would have employ'd me. I have heretofore fallen under the Resentment of large Bodies of Men, for refusing absolutely to print any of their Party or Personal Reflections. In this Manner I have made my self many Enemies, and the constant Fatigue of denying is almost insupportable. But the Publick being unacquainted with all this, whenever the poor Printer happens either through Ignorance or much Persuasion, to do any thing that is generally thought worthy of Blame, he meets with no more Friendship or Favour on the above Account, than if there were no Merit in't at all. Thus, as Waller says,

Poets loose half the Praise they would have got
Were it but known what they discreetly blot;

Yet are censur'd for every bad Line found in their Works with the utmost Severity.

I come now to the particular Case of the *N.B.* above-mention'd, about which there has been more Clamour against me, than ever before on any other Account. In the Hurry of other Business an Advertisement was brought to me to be printed; it signified that such a Ship lying at such a Wharff, would sail for Barbadoes in such a Time, and that Freighters and Passengers might agree with the Captain at such a Place; so far is what's common: But at the Bottom this odd Thing was added, N.B. *No Sea*

Hens nor Black Gowns will be admitted on any Terms. I printed it, and receiv'd my Money; and the Advertisement was stuck up round the Town as usual. I had not so much Curiosity at that time as to enquire the Meaning of it, nor did I in the least imagine it would give so much Offence. Several good Men are very angry with me on this Occasion; they are pleas'd to say I have too much Sense to do such things ignorantly; that if they were Printers they would not have done such a thing on any Consideration; that it could proceed from nothing but my abundant Malice against Religion and the Clergy: They therefore declare they will not take any more of my Papers, nor have any farther Dealings with me; but will hinder me of all the Custom they can. All this is very hard!

I believe it had been better if I had refused to print the said Advertisement. However, 'tis done and cannot be revok'd. I have only the following few Particulars to offer, some of them in my Behalf, by way of Mitigation, and some not much to the Purpose; but I desire none of them may be read when the Reader is not in a very good Humour.

1. That I really did it without the least Malice, and imagin'd the *N.B.* was plac'd there only to make the Advertisement star'd at, and more generally read.

2. That I never saw the Word *Sea-Hens* before in my Life; nor have I yet ask'd the meaning of it; and tho' I had certainly known that *Black Gowns* in that Place signified the Clergy of the Church of England, yet I have that confidence in the generous good Temper of such of them as I know, as to be well satisfied such a trifling mention of their Habit gives them no Disturbance.

3. That most of the Clergy in this and the neighbouring Provinces, are my Customers, and some of them my very good Friends; and I must be very malicious indeed, or very stupid, to print this thing for a small Profit, if I had thought it would have given them just Cause of Offence.

4. That if I have much Malice against the Clergy, and withal much Sense; 'tis strange I never write or talk against the Clergy my self. Some have observed that 'tis a fruitful Topic, and the easiest to be witty upon of all others. I can print any thing I write at less Charge than others; yet I appeal to the Publick that I am never guilty this way, and to all my Acquaintance as to my Conversation.

5. That if a Man of Sense had Malice enough to desire to injure the Clergy, this is the foolishest Thing he could possibly contrive for that Purpose.

6. That I got Five Shillings by it.

7. That none who are angry with me would have given me so much to let it alone.

8. That if all the People of different Opinions in this Province would engage to give me as much for not printing things they don't like, as I can get by printing them, I should probably live a very easy Life; and if all Printers were every where so dealt by, there would be very little printed.

9. That I am oblig'd to all who take my Paper, and am willing to think they do it out of meer Friendship. I only desire they would think the same when I deal with them. I thank those who leave off, that they have taken it so long. But I beg they would not endeavour to dissuade others, for that will look like Malice.

10. That 'tis impossible any Man should know what he would do if he was a Printer.

11. That notwithstanding the Rashness and Inexperience of Youth, which is most likely to be prevail'd with to do things that ought not to be done; yet I have avoided printing such Things as usually give Offence either to Church or State, more than any Printer that has followed the Business in this Province before.

12. And lastly, That I have printed above a Thousand Advertisements which have not the least mention of *Sea-Hens* or *Black Gowns;* and this being the first Offence, I have the more Reason to expect Forgiveness.

I take leave to conclude with an old Fable, which some of my Readers have heard before, and some have not.

"A certain well-meaning Man and his Son, were travelling towards a Market Town, with an Ass which they had to sell. The Road was bad; and the old Man therefore rid, but the Son went a-foot. The first Passenger they met, asked the Father if he was not ashamed to ride by himself, and suffer the poor Lad to wade along thro' the Mire; this induced him to take up his Son behind him: He had not travelled far, when he met others, who said, they were two unmerciful Lubbers to get both on the Back of that poor Ass, in such a deep Road. Upon this the old Man gets off, and lets his Son ride alone. The next they met called the Lad a graceless, rascally young Jackanapes, to ride in that Manner thro' the Dirt, while his aged Father trudged along on Foot; and they said the old Man was a Fool, for suffering it. He then bid his Son come down, and walk with him, and they travell'd on leading the Ass by the Halter; 'till they met another Company, who called them a Couple of sensless Block-heads, for going both on Foot in such a dirty Way, when they had an empty Ass with them, which they might ride upon. The old Man could bear no longer; My Son, said he, it grieves me much that we cannot please all these People: Let us throw the Ass over the next Bridge, and be no farther troubled with him."

Had the old Man been seen acting this last Resolution, he would probably have been call'd a Fool for troubling himself about the different Opinions of all that were pleas'd to find Fault with him: Therefore, tho' I have a Temper almost as complying as his, I intend not to imitate him in this last Particular. I consider the Variety of Humours among Men, and despair of pleasing every Body; yet I shall not therefore leave off Print-ing. I shall continue my business. I shall not burn my Press and melt my Letters.

2

Playing God and Playing for Power

For those living in colonial America, disease was a constant threat. In September 1690 *Publick Occurrences Both Forreign and Domestick* reported that already that year, 320 people in the Boston area had died from smallpox, but the epidemic was not as bad as the one 12 years earlier. In the epidemic of 1677–78, 700 residents—12 percent of Boston's population—died. When smallpox threatened again in 1721, hundreds of Boston residents left the town; of those families who remained, almost all had at least one member who contracted the disease.

On May 26, 1721, the Puritan clergyman Cotton Mather wrote in his diary that he planned to "procure a Consult of our Physicians" on the matter of inoculation against the disease although inoculation had "never been used in America, nor indeed in [England]." In spite of Mather's support for the procedure, only one of Boston's 10 physicians, Dr. Zabdiel Boylston, agreed to try it. However, his efforts caused as much consternation as the disease itself.

The *Boston News-Letter* printed a letter highly critical of the untried procedure in its July 17–24, 1721, issue. In response, Cotton Mather, joined by other Puritan clergy, published an open letter to the writers and to the community. The version included in this chapter is from the *Boston Gazette* of July 27–31. In that letter, Mather argued that inoculation would work and that the method should be viewed as a gift from God that should not interfere with people's faith in God or their submission to Him. But others were not convinced. To them, the new procedure appeared to be an example of people "playing God" on matters of life and death.

It is in this context that James Franklin began printing the *New-England Courant.* James, the older brother of Benjamin Franklin, has been portrayed as a champion of journalistic and religious freedom because he ignored the custom of publishing "by authority" and his *New-England Courant* carried many articles attacking the Puritan religious establishment. However, prominent members of the only Anglican church in Boston set Franklin up in the newspaper business because they saw the inoculation controversy as an opportunity to attack the Puritan clergy, undermine their authority and, with luck, make the Church of England the established church in the colony.

In contrast to other Boston newspapers, the first issue of the *New-England Courant* promised a witty and irreverent newspaper. However, the publisher's statement in the August 21, 1721, edition concluded with words signaling that the smallpox issue would be its main theme: "Pray hard against Sickness, yet preach up the POX!"

And "preach up the POX" the paper did. Both the *Boston Gazette* and the *Boston News-Letter* printed items relating to the controversy during the summer and early fall of 1721, but the *New-England Courant* had them in virtually every issue. It also kept the controversy alive even after the epidemic of 1721 ended.

The item attributed to Frank Scammony is an example of the issue-oriented letters printed in early newspapers. The "Dialogue between a Clergyman and a Layman," the second installment of which ran in the next issue of the *New-England Courant,* is a very early example of that form for presenting arguments. The objections to inoculation presented in the *Courant* are much like those used by religious people today who oppose procedures ranging from blood transfusions to abortions and cloning.

The final item is one of Benjamin Franklin's "Silence Dogood" letters. Like the other letters, it shows the influence of English essayists on the opinions and writing style of the young Benjamin Franklin. Because the letter in this chapter was published at the height of the smallpox epidemic, it very likely contributed to the inoculation controversy. Although other Silence Dogood letters were quite critical of the Church of England, in context this one was probably understood as an attack on the Puritan establishment. The "ingenious Political Writer" to whom Franklin refers is Thomas Gordon, one of the authors of the series known as "Cato's Letters." The letter containing the quote was published in the *London Journal* on May 27, 1721.

An Open Letter Defending Inoculation

The Boston Gazette, July 27 to 31, 1721

To the Author of the Boston News Letter

Sir:

It was a grief to us the *Subscribers,* among Others, of your Friends in the *Town,* to see Dr. *Boylston* treated so unhandsomely in the *Letter* directed to you last Week, and published in your Paper. He is a *Son* of the *Town* whom Heaven (we all know) has adorn'd with some very peculiar *Gifts* for the Service of his Country, and hath signally own'd in the Successes which he has had.

If Dr. *Boylston* was too suddenly giving into a new Practice and (as many apprehend) dangerous Experiment, being too confident of the Innocence and Safety of the Method, and of the Benefit which the Publick might reap thereby; Altho' in that Case we are highly obliged to any Learned and Judicious Person who kindly informs us of the hazard and warns against the practice, yet what need there of injurious Reflections and any mean detracting from the known worth of the Doctor?

Especially how unworthy and unjust (not to say worse) is it to attempt to turn *that* to his reproach, which has been and is a singular honour to him, and felicity to his Country? We mean those words in the Letter,—*a certain Cutter for the Stone*—Yes, Thanks be to GOD we have such a One among us, and that so many poor *Miserables* have already found the benefit of his great tenderness, courage and skill in that hazardous Operation cannot enough value the *Man* and give praise to GOD. And we could easily speak of *other Cases* of equal hazard wherein the Dr. has serv'd with such Successes, as must render him inestimable to them that have been snatch'd from the Jaw of Death by his happy hand.

The Town knows and so does the Country how *long* and with what *Success* Dr. *Boylston* has practic'd both in *Physick* and *Surgery*; and tho' he has not had the honour and advantage of an *Academical* Education, and consequently not the *Letters* of some *Physicians* in the Town, yet he ought by no means to be call'd *Illiterate, ignorant, &c.* Would the Town hear that Dr. Cutler or Dr. Davis should be so treated? no more can it endure to see *Boylston* thus spit at.

Nor has it been without considerable *Study expense in travel, a good*

Genius, diligent Application and much Observation, that he has attain'd unto that knowledge and successful practice, which he has to give thanks to GOD for, and wherein we pray GOD that he may improve and grow with all humility.

The mean while we heartily wish that Men would treat one another with decency and charity, meekness and humility, as becomes fallible creatures, and good Friends to one another and to their Country.

As to the *Case of Conscience referred to in the Divines,* we shall only say—What *Heathens* must they be, to whom this can be a question.

"Whether the suffering more the entire grounds of Machinations of Men, than to our Preserver in the ordinary course of Nature, may be consistent with that Devotion and subjection we owe to the All-wise Providence of GOD Almighty?"

Who knows not the profanity and impiety of trusting in *Men* or *Means* more than in GOD? be it the most learn'd Men or the most proper Means? But we will suppose what in fact is true among us at this Day, true Men of Piety and Learning after much *serious tho't* have come into an Opinion of the Safety of the faulted method of *Inoculation for Smallpox;* and being perswaded it may be a means of preserving a Multitude of lives, they accept it with all thankfulness and joy at the gracious Discovery of a *Kind Providence* to Mankind for that end:—And then we ask, Cannot they give into the method or practice without having their *devotion and subjection to the All-wise Providence of* GOD *Almighty* call'd in question? Must they needs *trust more in Men than in their great Preserver* in the use of *this means than of any other?* What wild kind of Supposition is this? and the *Argument* falls with the *Hypothesis* in our *Schools.*

In a word, Do we not in the use of all means depend on GOD's *blessing?* and *live* by that alone? And can't a devout heart depend on GOD in the use of this means with much Gratitude, being in the full esteem of it? For what hand or art of *Man* is there in this Operation more than in *bleeding, blistering* and a score more things in *Medical use?* Which are all consistent with a *humble Trust in our Great Preserver, and a true Subjection to His All-wise Providence.*

	Increase Mather
	Cotton Mather
Boston, July 27	Benjamin Colman
1721	Thomas Prince
	John Webb
	William Cooper

Frank Scammony Questions Inoculation

The New-England Courant, August 21 to 28, 1721

To the Author of the New-England Courant

Sir,

The story of *Inoculation* I see finds Employment for several Hands, some labouring to maintain, while others strive to destroy a base *Hypothesis.* And being of a public Nature, as most Disputes are, has given Birth to several Printed Speculations, which seem on one side not so much to defend the Practice, which was expected, and that justly, as on the other to condemn it as Mal- Administration, because disagreeing with the Modes of Physick, besides a little low Treatment on both sides. Verberations and Reverberations as if in Time they would look on one another, to be neither Christians nor Gentlemen, because they cannot agree in their Opinion.

A Distemper so awful as the *Small Pox,* could not but spread Fear and Amazement in and around a Place, which had escap'd a Visitation of so terrible a Nature so long. But the Concern, I observ'd, in some measure began to abate with some, upon the News of a much safer way of taking it by *Inoculation.* The Lawfulness and Safety of such a Practice was the next thing to be considered. *Two Select Men* of your Town, prudently conven'd, desiring the *Practitioners of Physick* to join them and give their Opinion on the Case before them; which they did, and after some Deliberation, it was unanimously agreed, saith my author (for I was not there) to be *rash and dubious, &c.* And in another Place he tells us, *B_____n* is desired by the Select Men to desist, and so 'tis thought were his Followers (or Directors which you please) *in an ordinary way.* I quietly submitted to the Decision of those whom I thought to be the properest judges; and thought no more of it for a time.

But some being inclin'd to countenance and receive the Practice, (which I imagin'd a culpable Transgression of the Charge given by the *Eybort,* and disputing the Opinion of the Judges) this I say, indue'd me to throw a few Reflections together, and see what I could find for or against it. Whether *Inoculation* might be admitted or not, in the Places under my Oeconomical Jurisdiction: And tho' they may be thought trivial, yet as they proceed from an honest Principle for the Publick Good, I hope they will prevail upon a disinterested Reader (and such I hope you are) to pardon their Intrusion.

I was puzzled a little at first to know how to state the Case, whether according to my own or the *Inoculating Plan,* but concluded to draw up both, and then both might be satisfied, they as well as my self.

The Case stated in my own manner was, *Whether Self-Infection was lawful.* I soon past it in the Negative: and my reason was, because I thought in the end it might prove a Species of Self-Murder, if the Infection carried me off; and I had no Assurance to the contrary, but it might.

The Case as it was stated by the Opponent Side is, *Whether it is unlawful to produce on one's Self a lesser Sickness to prevent a greater?* This, as it consisted of more Parts, requires more time for it's Resolution, at least a satisfactory & sufficient one, because several interrogatories are to be made, as Whether you are sure of having this greater *Illness* and whether mortal or not, and whether the lesser *Sickness,* as it is term'd, might terminate so, of which in these Places.

I look upon it very strange, believe me Sir, that there should be so many, who, blest with a sound and vigorous Constitution, should be desirous to bring upon themselves a *Distemper,* of which themselves are afraid, and from which so many flee, that they should be so discontented when God brings it upon them, yet can be very well satisfied to bring it upon themselves, after the new Fashion! We have been fore-acquainted with the fearful Effects and dangerous Consequences that have attended some who have undergone the *Operation,* of which we have had sufficient Testimonies, and which we are oblig'd to believe unless disapproved, and that after a better manner than affirming them to be *Industrious Reports, meer ungrounded Rumours,* and *uncertain Guesses.* You may as well persuade the Attestant he has no Eyes. It is a very weak way of disapproving Testimonies. If, I say, they have impos'd Falshoods upon the World, and you know it to be Imposition, then in Justice to the Operation, and its Followers you should have detailed it, otherwise it was not fair to force People to believe the contrary. If, after all the terrible Apparatus's presented to our view, or Evils which may reasonably be apprehended as Consequences of *Self-Infection,* we go on in an uncertain, insecure and dangerous manner, to hazard and endanger, what ought to be most dear to us, our own and our Neighbor's Life and escape: Let us *bless* God that he suffered us not to perish in the presumptuous way of our own Inventions, and own *it was of the Lords Mercies we are not consumed.*

But if we perish, what a Confluence of Evils are there, and at whose hands shall it be required? If *Infection* is communicated to another by means of *Self-Infection,* and this *Contagion* spreads it self among others, and any of those thus infected perish, at whose Hands shall their Blood be required? Since it was probable they might have escaped the *Natural Pock,* and thereby came to an untimely End.

Self-Love or Self-Preservation (the great Duty of the Sixth Commandment) is a universal Maxim or Principle, which the Great Creator has planted in the whole *Animal Creation;* it puts a Man upon seeking and securing that which is good, and avoiding that which is evil; it teaches him to seek *Health* and Safety, and to avoid Pain and Insecurity; for Pain and Insecurity must threaten our Preservation. It labours to find by what means *Health* may be made defensible, where the Approaches and Avenues to Danger lie open, and make suitable Preparations to let and hinder them, and all this in Subordination to the Divine Will and Rule.

The *Indispositions* and Ailments of *Human Bodies,* as they arise from several Causes, so have they several Ways and Means, as second Causes, for the Removal, and restoring to the *Body* a State of *Health,* to such a Degree as the Constitution of the Body is capable of receiving, or the Medicaments subordinately administered, are capable of conveying unto it, referring all to Him who is the Disposer of all things, and in whose Hands are the Issues of Life and Death. And he who neglects to use means when there is a Call for it, contributes so far to the destroying himself, as the neglected Remedies (if procurable) might have done him good. But *Epidemical distempers, as they more immediately proceed from a Divine stretched out Anon, and are sent as Judgments from an angry and displeased God, so they require a different Physick, a different* Way *of Prevention, Being the greatest Marks of the greatest displeasure, so they call for the greatest Humiliation, the greatest Observation of the Duties of Repentance.*

Thus our LEGISLATORS recommended in the *Proclamation for observing a Fast upon this Occasion,* which abounds with a true Christian Spirit and Concern, the very reading of which must needs affect a Soul (if capable of being mov'd) with a most awful Contemplation of the Divine Judgements, and excite a thorow Resolution, (with the Divine Assistance) to repent of and forsake those Iniquities, which have stirred up against us, the Wrath of an offended God. This, and this alone is the Prescription, even of God himself, to prevent his Judgments from falling upon us. This being observ'd, the Prophet then tells us, *Who knoweth but he may return and repent, and leave—Blessing behind behind [sic] him.* How far *Inoculation* suits with this *Directory,* and how far it helps us to *meet the Lord in the day of his Judgments,* is beyond my Ability to determine.

As *Boils* and *Blasms* are reckoned amongst the Judgments of the most High, what must the invading his Province be by bringing them upon our selves? If the Undertakers of *Inoculation* proceed after the Methods of those poor People mention'd, I adminish 'em to repent and forbear to *DIRECT AND MANAGE Small Pox* to any in such a Manner, than in an *ORDINARY WAY they shall be SURE OF NONE but a GENTLE VISITATION,* this with all Submission God Almighty never instructed poor People either to say or do, and therefore ought to have been rejected as an *Hypocrosie,* exceeding Christian Decency. I recommend to their Perusal the Judgment denounced *Deut. 28.17. The Lord thy God will smite thee with the Botch of Egypt, with the Emerods, with the Scab & with the Itch, whereof thou canst not be healed.* How far this may countenance an easy way of introducing what all good Men esteem a Judgment, I leave to be determin'd.

Men of Piety and Learning, Men whom I sincerely believe to be highly valuable and great for both, and whom I honour, may be perswaded that the *Inoculated Small Pox may be a Means for preserving a multitude of Lives,* but then are they perswaded that it may not be a means of taking away some? This wanted a *serious thought* as well as the other, but I had nothing of it. And unless I am perswaded that no such thing is to be fear'd, I shall be so far from *giving into* this Method and *Practice,* that I should think it ought rather to be call'd in Question.

It may be replied the *Artificial Pock* is not of that spreading *Infectuous* Nature. It may be; but I fear some may have experience'd the Contrary. This Gentlemen you should have consider'd before you proceeded to the *Practice.*

In short, I affirm it unlawful for a Person in *Health* upon any Account to receive a less *Infection* to avoid a greater, because Our blessed Saviour, the Great, the Skillful Physician says, *He that is whole needs not a Physician, but he that is Sick.* He allows of Application to Physicians in Cases of *Illness;* but *Health* has no need of Recourse to them.

As God blesses us with *Health,* by the sixth Commandment we are oblig'd to maintain it, and use it to the End bestow'd *to glorifie Him that we may enjoy Him forever.*

You say it is to prevent a greater *Illness,* how know you that you shall have any, much more a great One, or what you term a lesser Sickness may not result in the greatest, even that of the Death of the Soul for your presumptuous running into it. If you think you might escape it, why bring you it upon yourselves? If you thought you could not, why wait you not God's appointed Time, but must present to themselves the time *NOW* and the measure of but Invite a *GENTLE VISITATION AND THAT AVAILS Such.*

I am asham'd that these things of so pernicious Consequence, so destructive to *human Security* cannot be seen without pointing to 'em, and am sorry for so mean a hand. All I have more to say at present of the *Practice of Inoculation,* into which we are running, is serviceable and Lawful, and tends to *Preservation of a Multitude of Lives,* and endangers none, I question not not [sic] but 'twill have the Blessing of God and the Protection of the Government. But if it is unlawful and destructive of the Lives of the Liege subjects of his Majesty King GEORGE, His Excellency our Governor and the Senate of this Land, to whose Care and Government this great People is committed, and whose welfare they have so much at Heart, will, I hope, in their Great Wisdom and singular Prudence Judge and Determine the Affair.

Little-Compton   *I am, Sir*
Aug. 17, 1721   *Your very Humble Servant,*
                                        Frank Scammony.

A Dialogue between a Clergyman and a Layman, Concerning Inoculation

By an unknown Hand, *The New-England Courant,* January 1 to 8, 1722

Clergyman. The last Time I discours'd with you, you seem'd to discover a bitter Aversion to the new and safe Way of *Inoculation*; are you yet reconcil'd to that successful Practice?

Layman. I have but little reason to entertain a more favourable Opinion of that Practice than formerly, unless the Death of several Persons under the Operation of late, should induce me so to do. I confess, I am not yet convinc'd, that it is either a *lawful or successful* Practice.

Cl. The Ministers of the Gospel who are our Spiritual Guides approve and recommend this Practice; and they are great and good Men, who would not impose on the World, and surely, you ought to fall in with their Opinion.

Laym. I think the Ministers who have drove on Inoculation so fiercely have not only impos'd on others, but themselves also, so that we have reason to say in the Words of the Prophet (Hos. 9:7) *The Days of Visitation are come; —the Prophet is a Fool, and our Spiritual Men is mad.* I have abundant Reason to think, that they and I are equally ignorant of Inoculation, especially as to the *Success* of it; and if the Blind lead the Blind, both shall fall into the Ditch.

Cl. But why won't you believe the *Ministers*? They can explain the dark Passages of Scripture, and answer Cases of Conscience, better than *illiterate Men.*

Laym. I will believe no Man (tho' he be a Minister) because he is great and good; for such *may err,* and have sometimes deceived themselves and others: Nor have any of our Casuists as yet given satisfactory Answers to the Objections and Scruples which are rais'd against this upstart Way: But all the Books they have written for it (as *Moses* began his) they have fill'd with a *Chaos.*

Cl. Well, but you will acknowledge they are good Men, I hope.

Laym. They *are* or *should* be good; but I remember a great Divine says, "When we are about our Enquiry into Truth, let it be remembered; that neither the Great, nor the Learned, nor the *Good* are absolutely to be confided in."

Cl. But I find, *all the Rakes in Town* are against Inoculation, and that induces me to believe it is a right Way.

Laym. Most of the *Ministers* are for it, and that induces me to think it is from the D_____l, for he often makes use of good Men as Instruments to obtrude his Delusions on the World.

Cl. You must not say it is from the D____l because of the *Success* of it, for the D____l was never the Author of any thing for the Good of Mankind.

Laym. As to the Success of this Practice, the learned Dr. *Edwards* shall speak for me, and the rather, because Dr. *C. Mather (Bonif. p. 130)* says *More* Edwards *would be past Blessings.* "Some fool themselves into the grossest Errors by looking at that *Success* and *Prosperity,* and (as they are pleased to call it) the *Providence* which attends their Opinions and Ways. It is a Maxim among the *Turks* generally, that whatever prospers hath God for its Author: And so from their Success in their Wars, they have been wont to conclude that their Religion is from God, and owned by him. But I think the Scripture forbids us to learn the Customs of the Heathen.

Cl. Inoculation is not the worse because the Heathens first practiced it. They make use of Food and Clothing, and shall we reject those Gifts of Heaven, because they receive them? God forbid!

Laym. The Gift of Food and Clothing, which you bring for an Instance, is noways purtinent, for the Sixth Commandment requires us to use those things for the support of our Lives. Are you willing to indicate the Heathen in other Things besides *Inoculation?* The King of *Calesus* in the *East-Indies* lies not with his Queen in the night, but one of the Priests doth, who have a Gratuity bestow'd on him for that Service. I suppose it is not a worse Sin to break the Seventh Commandment than the Sixth.

Cl. I should be loth to conform to that outlandish Practice, because it is a mortal Evil, which I think Inoculation is not.

Laym. You do not think it is not a *mortal Evil,* for you cannot prove that it is not; none of you have done it as yet, and I presume you are all asham'd of your Craft, and will write no more in favour of the Practice.

Cl. I see you are obstinate, and will not be convinc'd. I will adjourn the Discourse to our next Meeting.

Silence Dogood on Hypocrisy

The New-England Courant, July 18 to 23, 1722

To the Author of the New-England Courant

It has been for some Time a Question with me, Whether a Commonwealth suffers more by hypocritical Pretenders to Religion, or by the openly Profane? But some late Thoughts of this Nature have inclined me to think, that the Hypocrite is the most dangerous Person of the Two, especially if he sustains a Post in the Government, and we consider his

Conduct as it regards the Publick. The first Artifice of a *State Hypocrite* is, by a few savoury Expressions which cost him Nothing, to betray the best Men in his Country into an Opinion of his Goodness; and if the Country wherein he lives is noted for the Purity of Religion, he the more easily gains his End, and consequently may more justly be expos'd and detested. A notoriously profane Person in a private Capacity, ruins himself, and perhaps forwards the Destruction of a few of his Equals; but a publick Hypocrite every day deceives his betters, and makes them the Ignorant Trumpeters of his supposed Godliness: They take him for a Saint, and pass him for one, without considering that they are (as it were) the Instruments of publick Mischief out of Conscience, and ruin their Country for God's sake.

This Political Description of a Hypocrite, may (for ought I know) be taken for a new Doctrine by some of your Readers; but let them consider, that *a little Religion, and a little Honesty, goes a great way in Courts.* 'Tis not inconsistent with Charity to distrust a Religious Man in Power, tho' he may be a good Man; he has many Temptations "to propagate *public Destruction* for *Personal Advantages* and Security": And if his Natural Temper be covetous, and his Actions often contradict his pious Discourse, we may with great Reason conclude, that he has some other Design in his Religion besides barely getting to Heaven. But the most dangerous Hypocrite in a Common-Wealth, is one who *leaves the Gospel for the sake of the Law:* A man compounded of Law and Gospel, is able to cheat a whole Country with his Religion, and then destroy them under *Colour of Law:* And here the Clergy are in great Danger of being deceiv'd, and the People of being deceiv'd by the Clergy, until the Monster arrives to such Power and Wealth, that he is out of the reach of both, and can oppress the People without their own blind Assistance. And it is a sad Observation, that when the People too late see their Error, yet the Clergy still persist in their Encomiums on the Hypocrite; and when he happens to die *for the Good of his Country,* without leaving behind him the Memory of *one good Action,* he shall be sure to have his Funeral Sermon stuff'd with *Pious Expressions* which he dropt at such a Time, and at such a Place, and on such an Occasion; than which nothing can be more prejudicial to the Interest of Religion, nor indeed to the Memory of the Person deceas'd. The Reason of this Blindness in the Clergy is, because they are honourably supported (as they ought to be) by their People, and see nor feel nothing of the Oppression which is obvious and burdensome to every one else.

But this Subject raises in me an Indignation not to be born; and if we have had, or are like to have any Instances of this Nature in New England, we cannot better manifest our Love to Religion and the Country, than by setting the Deceivers in a true Light, and undeceiving the Deceived, however such Discoveries may be represented by the ignorant or designing Enemies of our Peace and Safety.

I shall conclude with a Paragraph or two from an ingenious Political Writer in the *London Journal,* the better to convince your Readers, that Publick Destruction may be easily carry'd on by *hypocritical Pretenders to Religion.*

"A raging Passion for immoderate Gain had made Men universally and intensely hard-hearted: They were every where devouring one another. And yet the Directors and their Accomplices, who were the acting Instruments of all this outrageous Madness and Mischief, set up for wonderful pious Persons, while they were defying Almighty God, and plundering Men; and they set apart a Fund of Subscriptions for charitable Uses; that is, they mercilessly made a whole People Beggars, and charitably supported a few *necessitous* and *worthless* FAVOURITES. I doubt not, but if the Villany had gone on with Success, they would have had their Names handed down to Posterity with Encomiums; as the Names of other *publick Robbers* have been! We have *Historians* and ODE MAKERS now living, very proper for such a Task. It is certain, that most People did, at one Time, believe the *Directors* to be *great and worthy Persons.* And an honest Country Clergyman told me last Summer, upon the Road, that Sir John was an excellent publick-spirited Person, for that he had beautified his Chancel.

"Upon the whole we must not judge of one another by their best Actions; since the worst Men do some Good, and all Men make fine Professions: But we must judge of Men by the whole of their Conduct, and the Effects of it. Thorough Honesty requires great and long Proof, since many a Man, long thought honest, has at length proved a Knave. And it is from judging without Proof, or false Proof, that Mankind continue Unhappy."

I am, SIR, Your humble Servant,
SILENCE DOGOOD

3

The Great Awakening

A hundred years after the Pilgrims landed at Plymouth Rock, America was no longer as dangerous a place as it once was, but neither was it the New Jerusalem so many had envisioned. Immigration brought new churches to what initially had been religiously homogeneous communities. With prosperity came spiritual complacency.

Something of the encroaching spirit of irreverence and indifference can be seen in the "Dialogue between a Clergyman and a Layman" included in chapter 2. But by the time the Anglicans in Boston tried to wrest power from the dominant Puritan Congregational Church by setting James Franklin up in the newspaper business, the major threat to the established churches in New England was already well underway. That threat came not from free spirits such as James and Benjamin Franklin but from clergy who took their faith quite seriously.

During the 1720s and 1730s the teachings of ministers such as Jonathan Edwards, William Stoddard and William Tennent split churches into "Old Light" ones and "New Light" ones. Some of the points of contention between the two groups were the subjects for public debates of the kind noted in an item appearing in the *New-England Weekly Journal* on June 27, 1727. Those debates also set the scene for the first of many recurring periods of religious revivalism in America.

The Great Awakening, as this period of revivalism came to be known, was set in motion through the efforts of itinerant preachers such as James Davenport, Gilbert Tennent, the son of William Tennent, and, most notably, George Whitefield. For decades preachers had been lamenting both false doctrine and the indifference to all things spiritual they saw around them. Therefore, initially many of them welcomed these preachers into their communities. But others saw them as a threat.

The "Old Light" churches eschewed enthusiasm—the 18th-century term for the belief that emotions, impulses and intense feelings are to be accepted as revelations from God. Calvinist churches taught that some people are predestined to salvation and others are not. But the preachers of the Great Awakening encouraged a personal, enthusiastic and experiential religion. They taught that all people can be saved if only they will accept Jesus as their Savior and then lead a life in accord with biblical precepts.

This new message resulted in many converts. But it also divided communities, churches and even families into those who accepted the new teachings and those who did not. With the Great Awakening, the older denominations saw their power wane as Methodist and Baptist influence increased.

The stories in this chapter document the work of the Rev. George Whitefield, the most important revivalist of the Great Awakening. Oxford educated and a member of the Church of England, Whitefield was greatly influenced by Charles and John Wesley, founders of Methodism. At their urging, Whitefield first visited America in 1738 and 1739. Over the years Whitefield preached in most of the colonies, but his impact initially was greatest in New England.

The "Report on George Whitefield in New York" documents Whitefield's reception, his preaching style and its effect on his audience. As that report and the subsequent "Letter from a Writer in New England" indicate, Whitefield was a persuasive and very popular preacher. However, the letter taken from the *South-Carolina Gazette* also show the controversy surrounding his ministry because of the religious enthusiasm he promoted.

Those 1741 letters also illustrate how news from one region spread throughout colonial America. They were undoubtedly of great interest to Charleston residents because Whitefield had preached there in January 1740. The first page of the *South-Carolina Gazette* for December 19–January 5, 1740, had a handwritten note announcing Whitefield's arrival; subsequent issues carried reports of his work in South Carolina, which gave rise to lengthy theological debates that were published in the paper during February and March 1740.

During 1741 Whitefield's criticism of the faculty and students at Harvard and Yale provoked additional complaints from New Englanders. The commentary on that criticism outlines both Whitefield's charges against Harvard and the underlying doctrinal differences the Great Awakening brought to light. Whitefield, who had already left Massachusetts for England at the time critical letters began to appear in Massachusetts newspapers, responded with a letter that was published in the *Boston Gazette & Weekly Journal* on March 16, 1742. In it, he tried to mollify his critics, but with only partial success.

While Whitefield was in England, both support for revivalism and criticisms of it appeared regularly in newspapers from Massachusetts to South Carolina. On February 2, 1742, the *Boston Gazette and Weekly Journal* carried a testimony in which clergy thanked the Revs. Gilbert Tennent and George Whitefield for the revival of religion in their community; however, one year later, on March 28, 1743, the *Boston Weekly Post-Boy* carried an account of "religious excess" at New London, attributable to the Rev. Mr. Davenport and the "New Lights"; three months after that, on July 1, the *Boston Weekly News-Letter* reported Davenport had been expelled from Connecticut.

When Whitefield made his last trip to America in 1770, the personal, enthusiastic and experiential religiosity he taught met with new challenges from the rationalism of Enlightenment era thought that fueled the American revolution. A month after the *Massachusetts Spy* published the letter from Thomas Young, a Deist, and an August 25, 1770, reply to it, Whitefield died suddenly in Newburyport, Massachusetts. Newspapers throughout the colonies carried obituaries. Most of those obituaries, like the one from the generally critical *Massachusetts Spy* of September 29–October 2, 1770, praised his work.

A Report on George Whitefield in New York

The New-England Weekly Journal, December 4, 1739

The Rev. Mr. *Whitefield* arrived at the City of N. York on Wednesday the 14th Inst. a little before Night. The next Morning he waited on the Rev. Mr. *Vesey,* and desired leave to preach in the English Church, but was refus'd: The Reason assigned for such Refusal was, because Mr. *Whitefield* had no Licence to Preach in any Parish but that for which he was ordained; and an old Canon was read. To this Mr. *Whitefield* reply'd, That that Canon was Obsolete, and had not been in Use for above 100 Years, That the whole Body of the Clergy, frequently preach out of the Bounds of their Parishes, without such Licence. These Arguments not prevailing, some Application was made to the Rev. Mr. *Boel,* for the Use of the *New Dutch Church,* but this also was refus'd. Then Mr. *Whitefield* had the offer of the *Presbyterian Church,* but did not care at first to accept it, not being willing to give any Offence to his Brethren of the Church of *England*; but said, *He chose rather to go without the Camp, bearing his Reproach, and Preach in the Fields.* At length being informed, that in some Parts of this Country, the Meeting Houses had been alternately us'd by the Ministers of the several Communions, and very often borrowed by the Church of the Dissenters, he consented to accept the Offer for the Evening. However, in the Afternoon he preached in the Fields to many Hundreds of People.

Among the Hearers, the Person who gives this Account, was one. I fear Curiosity was the Motive that led me and many others into that Assembly. I had read two or three of Mr. *Whitefield's* Sermons and part of his Journal, and from thence had obtained a settled Opinion, that he was a Good Man. Thus far was I prejudiced in his Favour. But then having heard of much Opposition, and many Clamours against him, I tho't it possible that he might have carried Matters too far—That some *Enthusiasm* might have mix'd itself with his Piety, and that his Zeal might have exceeded his Knowledge. With these Prepossessions I went into the Fields; when I came there, I saw a great Number of People consisting of *Christians* of all Denominations, some *Jews,* and a few, I believe, that had no Religion at all. When Mr. *Whitefield* came to the Place before designed, which was a little Eminence on the side of a Hill, he stood still, and beckned with his Hand, and dispos'd the Multitude upon the Descent, before, and on each side of him. He then prayed most excellently, in the same manner (I guess) that the first Ministers of the *Christian Church* prayed, before they were shackled with Forms. The Assembly soon appeared to be divided into two Companies, the one of which I considered under the Name of GOD'S *Church,* and the other the *Devil's Chappel.* The first were collected round the Minister, and were very serious and attentive. The last had placed themselves in the skirts of the Assembly, and spent most of their Time in Gigling, Scoffing, Talking and Laughing. I believe the Minister saw them, for in his Sermon, observing the Cowardice and Shamefacedness of *Christians* in Christ's Cause, he pointed towards this Assembly, and reproached the former with the boldness and Zeal with which the Devil's Vassals serve him. Towards the last Prayer, the whole Assembly appeared more united, and all became hush'd and still; a solemn Awe and Reverence appeared in the Faces of most, a mighty Energy attended the Word. I heard and felt something astonishing and surprizing, but, I confess; I was not at that Time fully rid of my Scruples. But as I tho't I saw a visible Presence of GOD with Mr. *Whitefield,* I kept my Doubts to my self.

Under this Frame of Mind, I went to hear him in the Evening at the *Presbyterian Church,* where he Expounded to above 2000 People within and without Doors. I never in my Life saw so attentive an Audience: Mr *Whitefield* spake as one having Authority: All he said was *Demonstration, Life* and *Power*! The Peoples Eyes and Ears hung on his Lips. They greedily devour'd every Word. I came Home astonished! Every Scruple vanished. I never saw nor heard the like, and I said within my self, *Surely God is with this Man of a Truth.* He preach'd and expounded in this manner twice every Day for four Days, and this Evening Assemblies were continually increasing. On Sunday Morning at 8 o'Clock, his Congregation consisted of about 1500 People: But at Night several Thousands came together to hear him, and the Place being too strait for them, many were forced to go away, and some (tis said) with Tears lamented their Disappointment.

Letter from a Writer in New England to Friends in South Carolina

The South-Carolina Gazette, June 18, 1741

We have passed thro' a Winter the most tedious and severe in the Memory of Man: But neither that nor the Desolation of, are half so bad as sectarian enthusiastick Madness. *Whitefield's* Place has been occupied by his prime Friend *Gilbert Tennent.*—Their Prayers are generally censured as imperfect, immethodical, &c. But their Sermons and Expositions—! There from the latter you might hear yourself *cursed, damned, double-damned,* the Generality stiled *unregenerate, proud, Hypocrites, rotten-hearted, old Sinners, and Devils, and worse than Devils;* and these repeated and deliver'd in a long String, which would take many Minutes to bring out of his Mouth. This Creature has stirr'd the World, occupied almost all our Pulpits in Town, drawn off People from their necessary Labours every Day in the Week 2, 3, or 4 Times in the Day, at the Meetings, or more private Conventicles; neither Cold nor Rain, nor Snow, cou'd keep the red-riding-Hoods at Home by Night or by Day; groaning, crying, fainting took Place of regular Attention. Notes have been put up in great Variety and Number, even to 50 at a Time; for some 6 and upwards, some 12, some 30, 50, 60 Years old; some under Hardness of Heart, some wicked Children, some converted themselves for their unconverted Relations, some under Conviction, some half convicted. People are dissuaded and discouraged from the Sacrament, terrified, bewilder'd, distracted: And some after Agonies and Torments, like those of Hell, are happily recover'd and new born, *forsooth,* and with as much heavenly Joy as any *Bedlam* People. Boys and Girls from 6 Years and upwards take upon them to meet together for religious Exercises, and to go the Rounds, praying, conferring and exhorting. Several of the neighbouring Towns tally with us; *Cambridge* particularly, where great Numbers of the Students are taken off from all learned Improvements, and under the practical Whims of *Tennent,* whose Tutors find it impossible, to oblige them to their Exercises in these Times of prevailing Distraction; and I expect that impregnated with *John Bunyan, Stoddard, Sheppard &c.* they will soon get into the Pulpits, and fill the Country with *Antinomian* Reveries.

Commentary on George Whitefield's Criticism of Harvard

The Boston Gazette and Weekly Journal, April 20, 1741

To the Reader,

The Author of the following Remarks is a true and hearty Lover of the Rev. Mr. Whitefield, *thinks that he has been Instrumental in awakening and stirring up People to a serious Concern for the Salvation of their precious Souls; and it is the Author's daily Prayer that the Convictions and Awak'nings among us, may terminate in a sound Conversion, evidenced by newness of Life and new Obedience; but still he is not so blinded as to think that worthy Gentleman is infallible; and whoever reads his last Journal must be of the same Mind; there being many Things therein contained, and particularly with Relation to the* College *in* Cambridge, *and the Ministers of* New England, *without Foundation: And least this partial Account of the former, and his uncharitable Thoughts of the latter, should do as much Hurt to Religion as his Preaching did Good, the following Remarks are made.*

Mr. Whitefield observes, that on the 24th of *September,* he preached at the *College:* that it has one President, and four Tutors—Here his Account is partial, for he ought to have said that there are two Professors; one of Divinity, the other of the Mathematicks; as also an Hebrew Instructor; and he had added that these three Gentlemen were as well qualified for their respective Trusts, as any he ever conversed with, he would have spoke the Truth, and done the College but Justice.

He observes, that Discipline is at a low Ebb there; in which he is intirely mistaken. I lived at the College in two Presidents Time, both very excellent Men; the first particularly remarked for being a Man of Authority; and I am perfectly acquainted with the Government of the College at this Time, and so am as capable of knowing the Truth of that Matter as Mr. *Whitefield,* who never was at College but once in his Life, and then not a quarter of an Hour (except whilst a Preaching) and I do solemnly declare that I never saw the Authority of Government more maintained than at this Time, and I believe no one ever thought the contrary, saving this Reverend Stranger.

Again, he observes that the Tutors neglect to pray with and examine the Hearts of their Pupils; by which Account any one must necessarily suppose that they are in a worse State at College than the Heathens; for they have their publick Prayers: but here is a Society that call themselves Christians, consisting of above an Hundred Persons, and yet there are no public Prayers offered up to Almighty GOD for them, by those unto whose Care they are committed. But now is this the Case at College; no, the President prays twenty-eight Times a Week in the College-Hall, and the Professor of Divinity four Times; so that there are thirty-two Prayers offered up to God by the President and Professors every Week with and for the Students, who by Law are obliged to attend the same. *David,* a Man after God's own Heart, prayed Evening and Morning, and at Noon; which makes twenty-one Times in a Week: these Gentlemen pray two and thirty Times in a Week with the Students; and yet, there are no Prayers at College. Again, are not the Holy Scriptures read by the President twice every Day in publick, and often expounded by him? Hath not the Professor of Divinity three Lectures every Week upon the best and most important Subjects? Again, I do not see how it can be called a *Neglect* in the Tutors should they not pray with their Pupils; it was what was never done in good Mr. *Shepard's* Day, nor since the College had an Existence; they are not obliged by the Laws of the College to do it, which if it was tho't necessary, undoubtedly it would have been injoined them by the Corporation and Overseers; b[ut] if it is necessary, and yet not injoined them, the Legislative Power in the College are more to blame than the Tutors. Again, the Tutors praying with the Pupils is what I believe was never known in any University, especially where there are so many Prayers every Day as at the College in *Cambridge.*

But then how does Mr. *Whitefield* know that the Tutors do not privately talk with their Pupils, with respect to their Souls. I know the Tutors never told him they did not, I know he never had it from the Pupils, how then came he by his Knowledge; I conclude he argues it from this, he finds no Journal printed giving an Account of these Things, and therefore these Things cannot be. Private and personal Instructions, Examinations, Advice, and the like in their own Nature ought to be kept secret; and because I do not know that a Man does this or the other Thing, shall I therefore infer he doth not do it. I never heard any Man pray in secret, must I therefore conclude and report abroad that no Man makes Conscience of that Duty, because he doth not publish it. But in Truth I believe the Tutors do talk with the Pupils about their Souls as Occasion requires: I was when at College under Mr. *Flynt,* who to my certain Knowledge was very faithful as to that Particular, as well as all other.

Again, Mr. *Whitefield* is pleased to observe that bad Books are read, *Tillotson* and *Clark,* instead of *Shepard* and *Stoddard.* If he means by the Undergraduates, it is a Mistake, they do not read them; if he means the Graduates, I believe they do read *Tillotson,* and I hope they will, but not in the room and stead of Bishop *Hopkins,* Bishop *Peirson,* Dr. *Bates,* Mr. *How,* Dr. *Owen,* Mr. *Baxter,* and Dr. *Wates,* who were as Great and as Good Men as Mr. *Shepard* and Mr. *Stoddard;* these they could not read till lately, because out of print; and therefore if they read other Books as good, I hope they will be forgiven: and if they should read Dr. *Tillotson* also, I do not know that it would be a Crime. Those that censure him undoubtedly have read him; pray then allow others the same Liberty you take yourselves. There are a great many excellent good Things in Dr. *Tillotson,* that the Enemies to Dr. *Tillotson,* as I have heard some of them acknowledge, have got a great deal of Good by, and so many others. It certainly would have been better for Mr. *Whitefield* to have treated Dr. *Tillotson,* unto whom the Protestant Religion, and the Dissenters are so vastly indebted, as he has done the great Mr. *Stoddard:* He speaks very honourable and justly of him, and his Works, and recommends them; but then he thinking differently from Mr. *Whitefield* in some Things, about unconverted Ministers (where by the way Mr. *Stoddard* was perfectly right in my Opinion, as also in his Thoughts about unconverted Persons going to the Sacrament) is pleased to say of him thus—'That he honours the Memory of that great and good Man, yet he thinks he is much to be blamed for endeavouring to prove that unconverted Men may be admitted into the Ministry.' So I think Mr. *Whitefield* might have spoke of Dr.

Tillotson; might have recommended his Works in General, and cautioned the Scholars against his Errors, none of which were more destructive to Christianity (allowing Mr. *Whitefield's* Thoughts to be just about unconverted Ministers) then are Mr. *Stoddard's* Tho'ts and Writings upon that Subject. But again, there are in Dr. *Tillotson's* Writings Things fundamentally wrong (in Mr. *Whitefield's* Opinion) or there are not, if there are not, then no such Crime to read them; if there are, still they ought to be read by those capable of making a Judgment: Because Mr. *Whitefield* may be mistaken in these Things as well as Mr. *Stoddard* in other Fundamentals. And upon Supposition Mr. *Whitefield* should be mistaken, and Dr. *Tillotson* in the right, what will become of those that have neglected reading him, upon Mr. *Whitefield's* Prohibition; will that plead their Excuse in the Great Day? And as to the Students reading Dr. *Clark* and other Arian Writers, I believe they never did. True it is, that about the Year 1735, Dr. *Clark* and many Books much worse than his were read, and some were then given up to strong Delusions, and began to deny the God that bought them; immediately upon which the Divinity Professor laboured more abundantly in asserting and proving the important Truths then denied; and by the Blessing of God upon his learned and faithful Endeavours, a Stop was soon put thereto.

In short, Mr. *Whitefield* had no Advantages of knowing the true State of the College; never had any Account about the College from any Persons of Truth, and that were acquainted with it; provided he had no other Account, that what he has given in his Journal; and therefore what Regard can be had to it.

But before I leave the College, I beg leave to observe that by Mr. *Whitefield's* and *Tennent's* Preaching, there, the Scholars in general, have been wonderfully wrought upon, and their Enquiry now is, *What shall we do to be saved?* Some I believe have lately been savingly brought home to God: These Gentlemen have planted, Mr. *Appleton* hath watered; and a blessed watering it hath been: but after all, it was GOD who gave the Increase.

A Letter to George Whitefield from Thomas Young

The Massachusetts Spy, August 28 to 30, 1770

To the Reverend GEORGE WHITEFIELD

Sir,

A PUBLICK reproach will doubtless at least excuse a public complaint. In your lecture delivered at the Old North meeting-house on Wednesday evening, you were pleased to inform us, That Cain was the founder of the Deists, and gave this argument for proof, that because no blood attended his offering it was not accepted. If these be very material points in divinity, I should like to see them much better elucidated, than by a bare quotation of the opinion of a Reverend Doctor who, you informed us, put the matter out of dispute, that Abel also brought the fruits of the ground in offering. Should this Reverend Doctor have any collateral history of superior authority to that ascribed to Moses, he may perhaps from thence deduce irrefragable evidence to the point in question: but in the fourth of Genesis the story runs thus: *And Abel was a keeper of sheep, but Cain was a tiller of the ground. And in process of time it came to pass, that Cain brought of the fruit of the ground in offering unto the Lord. And Abel brought of the firstlings of the flock and of the fat thereof. And the Lord had respect unto Abel and his offering. But unto Cain and his offering he had not respect.* One would imagine that, from the previous account of the respective occupations of the brothers, their offerings were naturally supposable the fruits of their respective industry; and your large acquaintance with the sentiments of divines on this head, renders it needless for me to inform you, that the non-acceptance of Cain's offering has been very frequently ascribed to another cause. However, not to labor this matter, I presume if the hands of Cain had remained free from blood and violence *"not for the want of goats and bullocks slain,"* would God or man have been so much offended with him. There is [but] another difficulty, which the mist of antiquity hides from vulgar eyes, i.e. to come at any shadow of proof, besides the bare word of the Priest, that Cain was a person of any tolerable figure in religion at all, much less the founder of a set whose principles are the acknowledged foundation of every religion that has yet appeared in the world. The learned Dr. Samuel Clark, speaking of the Deists, acknowledges some classes of them to have right apprehensions of the natural attributes of God and his all-governing providence, in the direction of the affairs of men, as also, the obligations of natural religion, *justice, mercy and fidelity,* but so far only as these things are discoverable by the light of nature, without believing any divine revelation, and concludes, that the priinciples of those men are so immaterially different from those of christianity, that he questions whether such Deists exist. The compilers of the Universal History, however warmly they espouse the cause of Christianity, are diffuse in their encomiums on the excellent system of true religion, among the ancient Persians, which they acknowledge was refined Deism, or the pure unallayed religion of nature, flourishing in, and blessing that vast empire for many centuries. That these refined Deists are wrong in any tenet they profess is not pretended, even by their avowed opponents; the whole accusation against them is therefore reduced to a complaint, that there are some necessary truths they do not believe; the remedy in such case is only force; the several kinds of force, are brutal, perswasive, and rational: the first, thank heaven, is wearing a little out of fashion, the second loses ground, and unless we are forced by unquestionable evidence, and rational argument, to believe the Deity is inexorable by other means than cutting the throats and spilling the blood of innocent animals, we must remain with good King David and the ancient Persians, at least doubters of the absolute necessity of embracing our hands in blood in order to please our Maker.

I am, Sir, your humble servant,

THOMAS YOUNG.

4

Religion and Revolution

By the time of the Rev. George Whitefield's last visit to America in 1770, the colonies were moving inexorably toward a break with England. Instead of deferring to authority, newspapers began to assert their independence of it. Where once printer/editors described the purpose of their paper in religious terms, now they more often presented their papers as fulfilling political functions. Although they still published news items, letters and essays intended to promote true religiosity, their frequency decreased as the number of items using religion to justify or oppose a break with England increased. Justifications for the break came both from traditional Christianity and from Deism.

Most American papers took up the patriot cause. Cato's Letter, "Arbitrary Government proved Incompatible with true Religion, whether Natural or Revealed," first published in the *London Journal* on February 21, 1721, was widely reprinted in colonial newspapers. A supplement to the *Boston-Gazette* of March 22, 1773, promoted John Locke's essay on civil government.

Themes from those works appeared and reappeared in letters and essays by patriot writers, but often with a twist. Instead of tightly reasoned, scholarly arguments, patriot writings such as the "Commentary on the Stamp Act" reproduced from the *New-York Gazette* but also appearing in other newspapers including the *South-Carolina Gazette and Country Journal* of December 31, 1765, took on an impassioned, somewhat frantic tone.

Other essays gave vent to colonial dissatisfaction with England through the use of religious forms to make political points. "The First Book of the Marks" is an example of writings that borrow their structure and language from the Bible."The Geneology [sic] of a Jacobite," from the *Pennsylvania Evening Post* of February 9, 1775, and "The American Chronicles of the Times," published in the *Virginia Gazette* during January 1775, also use biblical style; "An English Patriot's Creed," published in the *Massachusetts Spy* on January 19, 1776, mimics the style of the Apostles' Creed.

Patriot newspapers also routinely published prayers, proclamations for days of prayer and sermons favorable to their cause. An example of a proclamation for a day of prayer, signed by John Hancock, can be found in the *Boston-Gazette and Country Journal* for July 3, 1775; a sermon delivered by the Rev. Gilbert Tennent appears in the *Massachusetts Spy* for December 4, 1776.

Although their writings suggest the patriots were convinced that God would be on their side as long as they remained faithful to his commands, they sometimes adjusted their religious practices to make them compatible with their political beliefs. The item from the *Virginia Gazette* announcing changes in the Anglican form of worship was picked up by the *Pennsylvania Evening Post* of August 3, 1776, and then by other papers around the country.

While the patriots used religion to justify their cause, those who sympathized with England argued that true religion and revolution were incompatible. In Tory newspapers, those arguments became more frequent as British fortunes waned. The essay reproduced in this chapter from Jeremy Rivington's *Royal Gazette* traces revolutionary zeal to the same misguided beliefs and hypocrisy that led religious dissenters to break with the Church of England. Those arguments show up again in the *Gazette* on November 25, 1778; a year later, on December 16, 1778, the paper reprinted an essay from a collection first published in London, in which the author also complains that "the pulpit has been shamelessly prostituted" by clergy who do not attend to "That part of scripture which inculcates loyalty." On October 16, 1788, the *Newport Herald,* edited by Peter Edes, reprinted an essay from the *Pennsylvania Packet* that linked revolution and the Anti-Christ. A Quaker testimony in opposition to revolution, based on that religion's pacifist beliefs, can be found in the *New York Gazetteer* for December 8, 1774.

Commentary on the Stamp Act

New-York Gazette, November 14, 1765

OH! inhabitants of New-York, and the British dominions in North-America: Hear my voice! Attend to the dictates of your patron,—your instructor—your companion—your friend;—The Genius of Liberty addresses you, oh! hear her voice.—

*—My origin is divine—I am co-existent with the Deity—My residence
was in his mind, before his divine benevolence had formed the design of
creation;—and I assisted in planning the glorious fabrick of the universe:* When God created rational intelligences, *and made* man *in his
own image;—the resemblance could not subsist without me; I gave* them
scope for the exercise of their *natural powers of action, and was the test
of* their *true characters: Without me vice could not be known, nor virtue
subsist:—Benevolence, generosity, gratitude, religion, love—could have
no place;—Nor without me could God or man ascribe either praise or
blame to any design or action;—A mere machine cannot be the object of
any resentment. Without freedom the whole universe must be a solitary
desart, filled with unmeaning machines, blindly performing, without design, the will of their Director; and he that gave them all their motions,
by irresistable impulses upon their minds, could never esteem and accept
their actions otherwise than as his own,—not the Creature's,—which being entirely passive, could neither receive his approbation or displeasure, nor be capable of reward or punishment:—God alone would be the
only actor in the universe;—and could he receive any pleasure in such a
forced obedience to his will? Could he esteem the creature who paid it
as an object of his love? As one that obeyed and adored him from gratitude and knowledge of the perfections of his nature? If these things
could not be, it follows that God has made freedom essential, and united
it to the very nature of man.* And what God has joined, let no man attempt to separate.

*As all men sprung from the same common parent, they were all origi-
nally equal, and all equally free—Every man had a right to do what he
pleased, provided he did not injure others who had the same rights as
himself. This regard to the rights of others was the only boundary to the
right of each particular. Whatever any one acquired, without injury to
others, was his own property; which none had a right to take from him.
When strength or cunning were employed to violate or encroach upon
the rights of others, it became necessary for* many *to unite in* defence *of
their properties against their invaders, Hence government arose. By
common consent some were chosen to act for the service of the rest, and
by each individual invested with his power, to render that service effectual.* The sole end of government was the publick good: *By the security
of private property, and the increase of the means of happiness—For the
more convenient collection of the power of a whole society or people, to
guard against or repeal the attempts of fraud and violence—To establish*

*prudent rules for the determination of property. To decide in difficult
cases, and accommodate justice to particular circumstances, so that
each one might enjoy his right; and to do whatever other matter should
be necessary to the publick good. It became also necessary to fix rules to
regulate the order and offices of government itself—These are various in
different places, but the design of all is the same, that is,* The publick
good. *So long as the end is pursued, the government is the peoples
friend—and it is their interest to support its offices and officers: But if it
happens, as it often does, that those who are invested with power and
authority to be employed for the publick good, make use of it to injure
and opppress their brethren, in direct opposition to the design of their
appointment—Then, if they cannot be removed, nor redress be obtained
by the ordinary methods of proceeding—the next consideration is,
whether the evils imposed upon them by those they have entrusted with
the administration of publick affairs, is greater than they would suffer
from the dissolution or suspension of government in its usual form. If the
latter is the least evil, then there always resides a power in the united
body of the people, sufficient to suspend or dissolve the powers they have
given, or oblige those who hold them to the performance of their duty.*

*This can only happen in cases that are very plain, and important to
the public, so that the whole body of the people concur in sentiment,
unite and determine as one man—Then they may naturally resume the
powers they gave—Powers that subsisted only in their consent to support
them—and take them again into their own hands, till their grievances
are redressed: for* the public good, *the sole end of government, is not to
be sacrificed to the form established, for attaining it.*

*It is needless to give cautions against this recurrence to the first prin-
ciples of government, but in cases important enough to justify it—for it
cannot happen at all but in such cases—without a discontent general
enough to occasion it, it cannot take place.*

*But as the Stamp-Act has given such an occasion for it, as never was
before known to Englishmen, which has excited more popular tumults
than ever till now happen'd in America, and, unless the fatal act, which
would utterly destroy liberty, is repealed, may yet occasion many more,
the effects of which may be terrible, unless properly regulated—*Some
advice upon that head, in case of any more such popular meetings may
be useful.

*All that compose such an assembly, especially those that act as lead-
ers and directors of the rest are advised, always to keep in mind, that the*

design of their meeting is to obtain a redress of grievances—not to occasion new ones,—therefore that no innocent person, nor any upon bare suspicion, without sufficient evidence, should receive the least injury.

They are advised to consider that while they are thus collected, they act as a supreme uncontroulable power, from which there is no appeal, where trial, sentence and execution succeed each other almost instantaneously—and therefore they are in honour bound to take care that they do no injustice, nor suffer it to be done by others, lest they disgrace their power, and the cause which occasioned its collection. Wherever there is power, there is an implied obligation upon it, to do justice and redress grievances; so that when the collective body of the people, for a time, take the power out of the hand of magistrates, into their own; the obligation upon them to do justice is no less than it was upon the magistrates, while the power was in their hands.

They are advised to consider that such extraordinary measures are only taken upon very extraordinary and important occasions; and ought to be confined to such weighty matters of general concernment and complaint, as could not be redressed by the ordinary forms of proceeding, nor admitted of any other remedy: That therefore the mixing any other matters of less general concernment or consequences, injures the grand cause of their meeting, and helps to frustrate the design of it.

They are advised to consider, that many men of bad principles will take the opportunity of publick commotions to perpetrate their base or villainous designs, to indulge revenge, or prey upon publick property, by leading heated tho' generally well-meaning multitudes, into actions that disgrace their proceeding, and weaken that power that is often of the greatest use, and the most terrible to arrogant, overgrown offenders, who have contrived to screen themselves from being brought to the punishments they have deserved, by the ordinary methods of proceeding; the greatest care therefore is necessary to keep an undisciplined irregular multitude from running into mischievous extravagencies: and if any enormities are committed, it damps the spirits of all concern'd, and perhaps may not leave them courage enought for the necessary defence of their liberties.

Lastly they are advised, as soon as the grand design of their meeting is fully answer'd, and security given that the Stamp-act, shall not be executed, immediately to dissolve—and let government go on in its usual form.

The First Book of the MARKS: A Commentary on the Stamp Act

South-Carolina Gazette and Country Journal, July 22, 1766

In our Gazette *of the eighth Instant, we gave our Readers the second, third, and fourth Chapters of the Book of the* Marks: *since which we have obtained the first Chapter, which we now publish, as thinking it may prove diverting to our Readers, although it does not come in proper Order.*

The First Book of the M A R K S

Chap. I

1. The Murmurs of the People, and the Division amonst them. 9. Speech of a great Man in their Behalf in the Sanhedrin. 17. The Rejoicings in the great City on Account thereof. 23. A further Destruction of the S***p-p***r.

NOW it came to pass that after the People had waited in Expectation of Relief from the mighty Men of the great House, even in the House of a great Assembly.

2. That they grew exceedingly weary, and were very wroth, insomuch that they returned their Ships, and their Goods, and would not let them pass this Way nor that Way, but sent them afar off, from whence they came.

3. And they worked each Man for himself, and each Woman for herself, and each Child for itself also.

4. And they made themselves Cloathing and Raiment to put on, even from the Produce of their own Land in great Abundance.

5. Now it came to pass when the great Merchants, and the Traders upon the mighty Waters, heard all that was done, they murmured amongst themselves, saying,

6. What now can we do? Our Ships and our Trade are at a Stand, and the Things that we have sent, behold them returned upon our Hands.

7. And their Complaints grew exceedingly high, for they wot not what to do.

8. And behold a great Man, even the Man of Wisdom and Integrity,

and one of the Number of the Lawgivers in the great House of the great City, rose up, and seeing the Burthens and the Troubles of the People, cried out with a loud Voice!

9. Men and Brethren! Ye perceive the Things that I long forewarned you of, that they are now come to pass, and the Peoples Oppression become very grievous before our Eyes.

10. Aforetime have I spoken again and again, but you would not hear, neither listen to my Words, or to the Prophecies I foretold.

11. Therefore is this Evil come upon you, and the Children of the Land made to cry out, Fie! Fie!

12. For their Trade is now stopped, and their Merchandise (the Glory of the East, yea, also, and of the South) is become even as Nothing.

13. Therefore I say unto you, take off the Burthen from their Shoulders; for the Poor crieth out in the Streets, and the great Men of your Trade go mourning all the Day long.

14. Thus spake the good Man for the Children of the C_____s, and for the Merchants, and for the Poor of the Land of Britain; yea for three Hours did he speak, and he gained Applause.

15. But it came to pass that while he was yet Speaking, G_____e, the Son of B_____l, rose up, and uttered many Things against this good Man, and against the Words which he had spoken.

16. But his Tongue was as the Tongue of the Wicked, and he made no great Weight with the Clacking thereof.

17. Now it came to pass that after these Things, a Report spread in the great City, that the Tax which had been laid on the People, would shortly be taken away.

18. And the Words of the good Man were made known unto them, and they rejoiced greatly thereat.

19. (For in those Days there were Scribes, and Men who did cunning Work with Types, and there were also Devils, and they made a great Stir in the City and in the Col_____es abroad, even unto America.

20. And when they had heard all that was done, they were exceeding joyful, and Gladness appeared in their Eyes, and they spake forth their Praises with Tongues of Gladness.

21. And behold the Musick in the Steeples, and on the Cleavers, and on the Parchments, were heard through every Street, and every Alley and Court.

22. And the Instruments of Wind, and the Fiddle were also heard; but the Bagpipe was not heard all the Day long.

23. Now the Children afar off heard not of these Things by Reason of the great Distance across the Land, and across the Sea.

24. And behold they were exceeding wroth, and they laid hold of one Caleb, and John, and George, and another John; and they demanded the Papers with the Marks on the Corner thereof.

25. And their Number was very great, so that they dared not refuse: So they gave unto them the Things they desired.

26. And behold on the second Month, on the fourth Day of the Month, that they laid them in a Heap, and set Fire thereto, and they burned then even to Ashes, so that not one of them was left unburnt.

27. And they made Figures of Straw, and of Rags, and they called them Masters of Stamps, and they burnt them also.

28. And behold when they had burnt all they could get, they departed joyful each Man to his own Home.

A Resolution Concerning the Anglican Order of Worship

Virginia Gazette, July 20, 1776

In C O N V E N T I O N, *July 5,* 1776

RESOLVED, that the following sentences in the morning and evening service shall be omitted: *O Lord save the King. And mercifully hear us when we call upon thee.*

That the 15th, 16th, 17th, and 18th sentences in the litany, for the King's Majesty, and the Royal Family, &c. shall be omitted.

That the two prayers for the King's Majesty, and the Royal Family, in the morning and evening service shall be omitted.

That the prayers in the Communion service which acknowledge the authority of the King, and so much of the prayer for the church militant as declares the same authority, shall be omitted, and this alteration made in one of the above prayers in the Communion service: *Almighty and everlasting God, we are taught by thy holy word, that the hearts of all rulers are in thy governance, and that thou dost dispose and turn them as it seemeth best to thy godly wisdom; we humbly beseech thee so to dispose and govern the hearts of the magistrates of this commonwealth, that in all their thoughts, words and works, they may ever more seek thy*

*honor and glory, and study to preserve thy people committed to their
charge, in wealth, peace, and godliness. Grant this, O merciful Father,
for thy dear son's sake, Jesus Christ, our Lord, Amen.*

That the following prayer, shall be used, instead of the prayer for the
King's Majesty, in the morning and evening service: *O Lord, our heavenly father, high and mighty, King of Kings, Lord of Lords, the only
Ruler of the universe, who doth from thy throne behold all the dwellers
upon earth, most heartily we beseech thee with thy favor to behold the
magistrates of this commonwealth, and so replenish them with the grace
of thy holy spirit, that they may always incline to thy will, and walk in
thy way; endue them plenteously with heavenly gifts; strengthen them
that they may vanquish and overcome all their enemies; and finally, after
this life, they may obtain everlasting joy, and felicity, through Jesus
Christ, our Lord, Amen.*

In the 20th sentence of the litany use these words: *That it may please
thee to endue the magistrates of this commonwealth with grace, wisdom,
and understanding.*

In the succeeding one, use these words: *That it may please thee to
bless and keep them, giving them grace to execute justice, and maintain
truth.*

Let every other sentence of the litany be retained, without any alteration, except the above sentences recited.

EDMUND PENDLETON, President

(*A copy.*)

J. Tazewell, clerk of the Convention

Seasonable Reflections on the Conduct of the Puritans

The Royal Gazette, January 31, 1778

It must afford astonishment to the honest, and thinking part of
mankind, that the conduct of those hypocritical fanatics, who brought the
best of Princes to the block, should still find advocates among a generous and enlightened people. But that astonishment will cease, when we
reflect that such as are now thus liberal in their censures of the unfortunate martyr, and are equally enthusastic in passing encomiums on his
murderers, would in our days, from the like spirit, as is plainly evinced

by their conduct, be as ready to dye their treacherous hands in the blood of their present sovereign.

A King, whose public and private virtues, are revered by all who are acquainted with his character, while from motives of venal opposition, blended with republicanism, in England, and ungrateful rebellious principles in the colonies, for the purposes of independency, ambition, fraud and rapacity; he is traduced with an appelation as ridiculous, as it is base. An appelation that tyrants only, who make their cruel sanguinary persecutions the test of justice, can apply to such a prince as George the third.

Taxation was the plea formerly—it is so now—But the great and primary source of rebellion at both periods, is to be ascribed to republican fanaticism. The multitude ever imposed on, merit our compassion. They are deluded, and inflamed to desperation and madness, by the puritanical trumpet of war: and the pulpit deum ecclesiastic. The humane therefore feel for their sufferings, but their leaders must excite indignation and resentment, in every loyal honest heart. By them the word of God is insiduously prophaned to promote persecution, desolation and distress, and to represent a prince conspicuous for his piety, as an object of divine wrath.

The good—the charitable, doctrines of the meek and humble Jesus, are impiously rejected, by pretended preachers of the gospel of Christ, while certain passages from the Old Testament are tortured to justify bloodshed, and to make the God of mercy, a pattern of rapacity, cruelty, and rebellion. To convince the public of the evil effects of puritanism and hypocrisy, I am warranted from history to observe, that these fanatics did all in their power to destroy the constitution as far back as the reign of Queen Elizabeth. Notwithstanding the patriotic zeal of that great Queen in defence of the Protestant religion, which depended almost entirely upon her for support. Notwithstanding her truly heroic spirit which has made the memory of Elizabeth dear to every honest Englishman, and revered by all good protestants, she repeatedly declared that she well knew how to please the Papists, but the Puritans she was sure neither God nor man could satisfy. The reason is obvious—It could not escape the pentration of an Elizabeth. She knew them to be

A Sect whose chief Devotion lies,
In odd perverse antipathies,
In finding fault with that and this,
And finding something still amiss.
                    HUDIBRAS.

That Queen was honoured by them with the name of *Hell's Empress. Supreme offender. Most bloody opposer of God's Saints,* and to compleat the catalogue, *most vile and accursed tyrant.* A name which these avowed enemies of monarchy, bestow as readily on an Elizabeth, or a George, as on a Nero or a Caligula.

Such was the disquietude they gave to James the first, from their rancour to Kings, and to episcopacy, that this judicious monarch, in the advice he gives to his son Charles, expresses himself in the following manner, "Take heed of all Puritans, for they are aspiring without measure, and make their own imagination the square of their consciences." A trite and just definition of the character of these fanatics, entirely agreeing with the many witty lines thrown out against them in Butler's Hudibras.

A Poem that must render the memory of Puritans despicable to posterity, so long as truth shall find advocates, fanatical hypocrisy excite detestation, and wit and humour be admired.

In the reigns of Queen Elizabeth, and King James the first, these professed enemies to kingly government, were happily foiled in their base and treasonable endeavours against the state. But the substituting a republic and calvinistical principles of religion on the ruins of the established government, being the grand object of their policy. An object which could not be effected without the destruction of all that was held sacred in the church and state. They were therefore determined to avail themselves of cant and hypocrisy, which will ever prevail with the multitude, in a bigotted age, and by such base and iniquitous means, they at length gained their end. Hence the martyrdom of that virtuous Prince, Charles the first, and hence to the lasting infamy that must await on his murderers.

A Prince, whose memory, when we allow for the difficulties he had to combat, the undefined prerogatives of the crown, and the treachery of his enemies, must be reverenced by the wise and the honest, whatever the knave, the fool, and the deluded bigot may say to the contrary.

A rebellion, the evil effects of which, are alas! but too severely felt at this time in America, from the pernicious influence of a fanatical priesthood; joined to the detestable machinations of designing demagogues, whose ancestors, in the last age, deluged Great-Britain with blood, and whose descendants are now, from the same motives, determined to rival them, by introducing the like miseries in this once happy, but now truly wretched country.

PACIFICUS

5

Disestablishment and Its Discontents

With independence from England came the need to find a way to create a united nation from 13 colonies, each with different needs, cultures and concerns. For the fledgling nation, what to do about religion was, perhaps, the most difficult question. Although philosophers of the era often linked religious and political freedom, the meaning and extent of that freedom became subjects for much public debate.

Some who supported the patriot cause firmly believed a common religion to be a necessity for peace, national unity and stability. In the essay from the *Massachusetts Spy* reproduced in this chapter, Worcestriensis argues that position most clearly. In the installment published in the next issue, he acknowledges the argument against an established religion, but finally concludes government has a duty to do what is necessary to promote national unity and protect people from error.

For others, safety and security seemed to lie in complete religious freedom and equality. Anything else was somehow un-American. In a satirical piece published in the June 1, 1776, *Pennsylvania Evening Post* over the names "Hutchinson, Cooper, Cato, &c. &c.," the authors give as two of 11 reasons for opposing independence from England:

> 7. The church will have no King for a head.
> 8. The Presbyterians will have a share of power in this country. N.B. These people have been remarked, ever since the commencement of our disputes with Great-Britain, to prefer a Quaker, or an Episcopalian, to one of their own body, where he was equally hearty in the cause of liberty.

Meanwhile, Virginia's representatives adopted a Declaration of Rights that, among other things, guaranteed religious freedom. The Declaration was duly published in the *Virginia Gazette* on May 24, 1776. It was reprinted on June 6, 1776, in the *Pennsylvania Evening Post,* where it became one more thing to consider by Pennsylvanians as they debated a new frame of government.

In installments that ran in the *Pennsylvania Evening Post* from October 10 through October 31, 1726, Orator Puff and Peter Easy debated every aspect of that new frame of government. The segment in this chapter presents arguments for and against removing religious tests for public office, which was among the most controversial of the proposed provisions. From June through October of that year, Philadelphia newspapers were filled with arguments supporting and opposing elimination of religious tests.

Although Pennsylvania was one of the few colonies that had never had an established religion, its laws had required that those serving in government be Christian. Rhode Island, founded on the principle of complete religious freedom by Baptists who had been driven from Massachusetts, was the most consistent supporter of complete freedom for Christians, non-Christians and nonbelievers alike. As early as January 11, 1733, the *Rhode-Island Gazette* carried essays making the case for a system like theirs where, "We have even no Terms of Reproach, and are burdened with no Establishment." After the state's convention debated the new Constitution for the United States, the *Newport Herald* of June 3, 1790, published the convention's sentiments, which included demands for "certain actual rights" including religious freedom. In the year before the Bill of Rights was finally adopted, Rhode Island papers published many exchanges like the one in this chapter between the Jewish community and President George Washington. As with an earlier petition from the Quaker community, published in the *Newport Herald* on October 29, 1789, the religious minority sought assurance their interests would be protected.

With the adoption of the First Amendment in 1791, debates over religious freedom temporarily died down. However, they quickly flared up again. The elections of 1798 and 1800 were among the most bitterly fought, dirty campaigns in American history. Religion, as much as politics, was the issue.

As war between England and France loomed, the federalists, who were in power, saw safety in siding with England. To them, the French Revolution appeared excessively violent and radical; they labeled the French, and the anti-federalists at home who generally sided with France, as atheists. In return, the anti-federalists accused the English-sympathizing federalists of wanting to restore the monarchy and establish the Church of England as the religion of the land.

In early salvos from New York, writers for the federalist *Gazette of the United States* launched attacks on Benjamin Franklin during late May and early June of 1796. Before providing a more complete defense of his grandfather's lifestyle and religious beliefs on June 15, Benjamin Franklin

Bache wrote in his Philadelphia *General Advertiser (Aurora)* on June 11, 1796:

> The private characters and conduct of men have never with propriety been dragged before the tribunal of the press; . . .
> . . . is a man to be judged incapable of sharing in the management of the finances of a country, because an infamous debauchee; or is another to be adjudged unworthy of an eminent station in a republic, because a brutal tyrant in his house?

But Bache was not above attacking his political opponents. Throughout the period, anti-federalist newspapers, and most notably Benjamin Franklin Bache's *General Advertiser,* kept up a steady stream of attack on the federalists. Their view that a vote for federalists meant a vote for a return to the monarchy and an establishment of religion can be seen most clearly in "Religious Tyranny Yet Practiced," which contains an extract from a work by the Quaker William Penn. When President John Adams, fearing the United States would soon be at war, called for a day of repentance and prayer, Bache devoted much of the March 30, 1798, issue to criticism of President Adams for his supposed monarchical tendencies and religious hypocrisy. While the item reproduced in this chapter comments more generally on public prayer in behalf of political interests, "A good Christian and Enemy to hypocrisy" wrote, in response to the president's proclamation:

> . . . to the President and Ministers *alone* can be applied these terrible words of the proclamation, that *the just judgments of God against prevalent iniquity are a loud call to repentance and reformation.* The good American people are only guilty of one fault . . . *it is that of having elected Mr. Adams their President.*

The federalist attacks on Thomas Jefferson for his unconventional religious beliefs are well known. Some examples can be found in July and August 1798 issues of John Fenno's *Gazette of the United States* and Noah Webster's *Minerva.* The article included in this chapter is somewhat unusual because it appeared in papers that are not usually associated with the party press of the era and because the writer attacks Jefferson's behavior with respect to religion as much as his religious beliefs.

The Need for a Common Religion with Limited Tolerance for Others

The Massachusetts Spy, August 21, 1776

For the MASSACHUSETTS SPY.
American Oracle of Liberty. NUMBER III.

"A serious attention to obtain in all our action the approbation of an infinitely wise being cannot fail of producing excellent citizens. For rational piety in the people, is the firmest support of a lawful authority. It is in the rulers heart, the pledge of the people's safety, and produces their confidence."   *VATTEL'S LAW, &c.*

To the Hon. LEGISLATURE *of the* STATE *of* MASSABHUSETTS [sic] BAY.

FROM the observation of stubborn facts we have undeniable proof that the practice of virtue and religion has a direct tendency to increase the felicity of a Nation or State.

By the word *religion* we are to understand the knowledge of divine things relative to the *other* world, together with a practice conformable thereto, and conscientious observance of the rites and ordinances of that worship which is best calculated for, and expressive of the honor and glory of the *great Governor* of the Universe.

In my last I endeavoured to prove the great utility and absolute necessity of establishing the means of good *education* in the State.

This must preceed the knowledge of religion, if we would begin at the right end. The knowledge of our duty must be obtained before the practice of it can take place. Next to *that,* it is incumbent on the conductors of a state to use the most probable means of instilling religious sentiments into the people under their care and direction. Every individual member of the State is indispensibly bound to obtain an acquaintance with the *Supreme Being,* and the relation he stands in to him, and also to maintain sentiments worthy of the dignity *of his* nature, that so proper homage love and submission to his will may be exhibited.

Now if every member is thus bound, the whole state of course must be under the same obligation. Hence the *rulers* of a people, above all others, ought to be continually under the influence of religion. On them is the public *eye* and their example is destructive, or beneficial proportunately as they are vicious, or virtuous. "Ye masters of the earth (says Vattel) who acknowledge no superior here below, what assurance can your subjects have of your intentions, if they do not see you filled with respect for the common father and lord of men and animated with a desire to please him?

Hereby they will not only secure to themselves the felicity resulting from the peace of their own minds, but also will much facilitate the performance of the duties of their office, by being patterns and examples of a rational and regular deportment.

So far as the religion of Subjects comes within the jurisdiction of public authority, the rulers of the State are indispensibly bound to exercise their utmost care and vigilance in the establishment and support of it. Rulers were appointed to promote the happiness of the people: This design respects their internal as well as temporal State, the felicity of a State results, in part, from the regularity and good orderance of its *internal police*. Therefore religion ought to be propagated and promoted, in as much as it causes men to yield a more chearful submission to good and wholesome laws; to act with fidelity in their dealings with their neighbour, and renders them "more firmly attached to their country." The rites and ordinances of religion very much affect the manners of men, and of consequence the felicity of the State. In respect of the eternal happiness of mankind, religion is of infinite importance, and therefore of right comes under cognizance and claims the protection and support of the directors of the common wealth.

Where there is no religion, there society is destitute of its strongest cement: Without it oaths have no solemnity nor force; a horrid train of consequences ensue, which have a most malignant influence upon Society.

But while we recommend to the conductors of this State a strict attention to the promotion of religion, we intend not, we deprecate a zeal not according to knowledge. A rational religion, void of fanaticism and superstition, alone ought to be countenanced. When narrow Principles and a persecuting spirit prevail, miserable is the State of that people among whom they display their horrid Glare.

But it must be remembered that it is only the External part of religion that comes under the legal cognizance of the State. We are entirely independent in matters which concern our consciences; our belief and worship are not under the controul of human power; we are answerable to the Deity only for our faith, to our own master we stand or fall.

For "every mans private persuasion or belief (as the Learned Dr.

FURNEAUX observes in answer to BLACKSTONE) must be founded upon evidence proposed to his own mind; and he cannot but believe, according as things appear to himself, not to others; for his own understanding, not to that of any other man. Conviction is always produced by the light which is struck into the mind; and never by compulsion, or the force of human authority."

Hence it follows that the Legislature of a State have no controul over the minds of men, in regard to their religious principles and belief. Therefore it is consistent with the best Policy, and is the most equitable proceedure, to give an universal TOLERATION of all religions, the principles and practice of which do not operate to the disadvantage and ruin of the Common wealth.

The reason why any particular religion should not be tolerated is not because *we,* or our *Rulers* may think it unscriptural or absurd; but because it militates with, and has a direct tendency to sap and undermine the foundation of State government.

The Romish Catholic religion is disallowed and proscribed, not so much because it contains a *Farrago* of Monstrous absurdities and contradictions, as because it is professedly and practically a distinguishing tenet, principle, and characteristic of the papists, that the ecclesiastical is above the civil power, that the *Church* is authorised to depose *evil rulers* at pleasure; and that to kill and destroy all, who differ from them in religious Sentiments, is no crime.

Properly to discuss this important Subject, opens a wide Field, and must be our business in another paper.

WORCESTRIENSIS.

(*To be continued.*)

A DIALOGUE between Orator *Puff* and *Peter Easy,* on the Proposed Plan or Frame of Government

The Pennsylvania Evening Post, October 15, 1776

Peter. Will not the people, and especially the clergy, be exceedingly alarmed to think in the midst of so dreadful a war, that we have, *by the public authority* of so great a State passed such strongly implied censures of contempt on our holy religion, and *weakened the securities of it by law establishment,* while, at the same time, we are continually imploring the assistance of heaven in supplications and form of that religion. Is not this hypocrisy? The former qualifications required by law was a positive, clear, direct, *"profession of the Christian faith."* It admitted of no gloss or equivocation. How can we ask or expect success, while we thus deliberately, in the face of the whole world, are undermining the religion graciously delivered to us by Heaven, with such amazing circumstances of mercy? I tremble at the thought. I most fervently hope this article will be altered when the new Assembly meets, that is to be chosen next *November.*

Orat. I tell thee it is impossible. That Assembly will have no powers but what are assigned to them by the Frame of Government; and the power of *altering* any part of the Constitution is not assigned to them, but is positively reserved to the Convention alone, that may be called *nine years hence.* If the Assembly could alter *one* part they might alter *another,* and so undo all the labors of our leaders; but they were too wise to leave that door open, and have thoroughly guarded against such an evil. Here—read the last lines of the preamble to the Declaration of Rights, &c. where the last Convention says, "We do, by virtue of the authority vested in us by our constituents, ordain, declare, and *establish* the following *Declaration of Rights* and *Frame of Government* to be the CONSTITUTION of this commonwealth, and to *remain in force therein forever,* except in such articles as shall hereafter, on experience be found to require improvement, and which shall by the same authority of the people, fairly *delegated* AS THIS FRAME OF GOVERNMENT DIRECTS, be amended," &c. that is by a Convention, called by a Council of Censors, which *cannot* be till *nine years* hence, as is *expressly* provided by the last section of the Frame. Again, in the *ninth* section, the Conventions says *positvely* in mentioning the powers of the Assembly——"But they shall have *no power* to *add* to, *alter, abolish, infringe any part* of this Constitution." Indeed, I hope the late Convention has used words of such force that no Assembly or Convention to the end of time will have power to alter the *grand alteration* [t]hey have made; for they have used words on this point of *religion* which they have not on any other article. See the *tenth* section, where they say "and no *farther* or *other* religious test shall *ever hereafter* be required of any civil officer or magistrate in this state." This Frame is so calculated to coax the people, and it is to be so speedily carried into execution, that it cannot be opposed; and at the end of nine years, if we are successful, people will think religion is of no consequence in military operations. Now, *Peter,* however amazing these alterations in the qualifications of officers, and consequently this new RELIGIOUS FOUNDATON for our new commonwealth, are, yet, supporting one thing, thou must acknowledge the ingenuity and courage of our statesmen deserve admiration, if not esteem.

Peter. How so?

Orat. Why, suppose some of our statesmen do not like the religion profest in this country; suppose they do not think it *simple* enough, and they should be afraid that *their sentiments on this subject are well known*; how confoundedly must they have been gravelled, if they had not made this change?

Peter. What difficulty would they have been under?

Orat. Why, if the ancient declaration of *"faith"* were to be taken by every Member of Assembly, &c. such men must either refuse to take them, and thereby throw themselves out of power, or else take from time to time as often as required, and so by frequently and solemnly affirming to believe in a religion of which they did not believe a thing, draw down upon themselves the reproaches and detestation of all worthy men, who should *know their real sentiments.* Whether this is the case, I leave thee to judge from facts. Certain it is, that those inhabitants of this state, who do not believe the *Christian* religion, would have been very well off, if they had only been allowed a TOLERATION, and been permitted to live undisturbed; and therefore they are under the greatest obligation to our statesmen, who have put it into their power to hold the *highest offices* in the government, and both to *make* laws and to *execute* them. The *Christian* religion, *Peter,* has subsisted near eighteen centuries—*Peter,* near eighteen centuries—a long while—a very long while. Time alters opinions, *Peter,* thou knowest—as the poet says.

"We think our fathers *fools,* so wise *we* grow;
Our wiser sons no DOUBT will think us so."

Peter. However, there seems to be no great likelihood of any large number of persons getting into offices of power, who do not believe our religion, as long as the inhabitants in general continue *Christian.*

Orat. Ah, *Peter,* that is true; but thou art no politician—thou dost not comprehend the *mighty influence* which the FOUNDATIONS of a frame of government, as to religion, gradually produce in the minds of men. In a few years men may argue in this manner—"What could induce the *patriotic* and *wise* Convention of *Pennsylvania* that modelled this commonwealth in the year 1776, in so *wonderful* a manner as to excite the *astonishment* of all *America,* what could persuade that *learned, illustrious,* and *venerable* body, to alter the *old religious regulations* as to offices in government, and to put the *Christian, Jewish,* and *Mahometan* religions with respect to them on the same footing? Is no regard due to those *enlightened fathers* of their country? And must not they have had convincing reasons to have urged them to pass so slightly over the *Christian* faith? Must not they have been persuaded, that the *public welfare would be best promoted* by this surprising INNOVATION? Why else would they have acted in this manner? And if the public welfare will be *best promoted* by this extraordinary political refinement, can it be prejudicial to our souls? *That* is impossible: For the establishment that *best promotes the public welfare,* must be *best* in every respect." May not this lead people, *Peter,* to think with more indifference of the *Christian* religion than they used to do? Oh, *Peter,* great things may arise from this step of our Convention. They are, many of them, bright men—They see far into futurity. It must be acknowledged that the *Christian* religion some how or other discourages many bold exertions of the human mind. *Rome* and *Athens, Peter,* were not *Christian* commonwealths.

[*To be continued.*]

The Jews of Rhode Island Welcome the President, with Reply from George Washington

The Newport Herald, September 9, 1790

AN ADDRESS.

To the PRESIDENT *of the* UNITED STATES *of* AMERICA.

SIR:

PERMIT the Children of the Stock of Abraham to approach you with the most cordial affections and esteem for your person and merits—and to join with our fellow-citizens in welcoming you to Newport.

With pleasure we reflect on those days—those days of difficulty and danger, when the GOD of Israel, who delivered David from the peril of

sword—shielded your head in the day of battle:—And we rejoice to
think, that the same spirit, who rested in the bosom of the greatly
beloved Daniel, enabling him to preside over the provinces of the Baby-
lonish Empire, rests and ever will rest, upon you, enabling you to dis-
charge the arduous duties of CHIEF MAGISTRATE In these States.

Deprived as we heretofore have been of the invaluable rights of free
citizens, we now (with a deep sense of gratitude to the Almighty Disposer of all events) behold a Government, erected by the MAJESTY OF
THE PEOPLE—a Government which to bigotry gives no sanction—to
persecution no assistance; but generously affording to ALL liberty of
conscience and immunities of citizenship—deeming every one, of whatever nation, tongue, or language, equal parts of the great governmental
machine. This so ample and extensive Federal Union, whose basis is
philanthropy, mutual confidence, and public virtue, we cannot but acknowledge to be the work of the GREAT GOD, who ruleth in the armies
of heaven and among the inhabitants of the earth, doing whatsoever
seemeth good.

For all the blessings of civil and religious liberty which we enjoy under an equal and benign administration, we desire to send up our thanks
to the Ancient of Days, the great Preserver of men—beseeching him,
that the Angel who conducted our forefathers through the wilderness into
the promised land, may graciously conduct you through all the difficulties and dangers of this mortal life; and when like Joshua, full of days
and full of honor, you are gathered to your Fathers, may you be admitted
into the Heavenly Paradise to partake of the water of life, and the tree of
immortality.

Done and signed by order of the Hebrew
Congregation *in* Newport, *Rhode-Island,*
August 17, 1790.

MOSES SEIXAS, Warden

The PRESIDENT's ANSWER

To the HEBREW CONGREGATION *in Newport,* Rhode-Island

GENTLEMEN:

While I receive with much satisfaction, your Address replete with expressions of affection and esteem, I rejoice in the opportunity of assuring
you, that I shall always retain a grateful remembrance of the cordial welcome I experienced in my visit to Newport, from all classes of citizens.

The reflection on the days of difficulty and danger which are past, is rendered the more sweet, from a consciousness that they are succeeded by days of uncommon prosperity and security. If we have wisdom to make the best use of the advantages with which we are now favored, we cannot fail, under the just administration of a good government, to become a great and happy people.

The citizens of the United States of America, have a right to applaud themselves for having given to mankind examples of an enlarged and liberal policy—a policy worthy of imitation. ALL possess alike liberty of conscience, and immunities of citizenship. It is now no more that toleration is spoken of, as if it was by the indulgence of one class of people that another enjoyed the exercise of their inherent natural rights. For happily the government of the United States, which gives to bigotry no sanction—to persecution no assistance, requires only that they who live under its protection, should demean themselves as good citizens, in giving on all occasions their effectual support.

It would be inconsistent with the frankness of my character not to avow, that I am pleased with your favorable opinion of my administration, and fervent wishes for my felicity. May the Children of the Stock of Abraham, who dwell in this land, continue to merit and enjoy the good will of the other inhabitants; while every one shall sit in safety under his own vine and fig-tree, and there shall be none to make him afraid. May the Father of all mercies scatter light and not darkness in our paths, and make us all in our several vocations useful here, and in his own due time and way everlastingly happy.

GEO. WASHINGTON

Religious Tyranny Yet Practiced in Certain Parts of the United States

The General Advertiser (Aurora), November 4, 1796

For the AURORA.

The friends of undefiled religion and especially those, who have suffered grievous persecutions *for conscience sake,* ought to be particularly serious at this juncture. We are about to choose a Chief Magistrate and it is due to our Divine Maker himself, as well as to our Fellow Men, that we have a watchful, serious care of religious liberty.—Isaac Backus, a minister of the Baptist society in Massachusetts government, published *in June last* a continued account of many religious sufferings and impositions in that quarter, down to the present year, 1796.—Such things at this time of day would not be credited upon common authority; but certainly we must yield our sorrowful belief to facts openly stated in a volume of 300 pages in Boston, with the author's name about the impiety of the laws of that state, in imposing religious taxes and compulsions. At this time a single extract (page 302) must suffice. The book requires the reading of every good and prudent freeman of America.

EXTRACT.

"But as this has restrained our legislature from making any certificate law to exempt the dissenters from the congregational denomination from taxes to the worship, and they have put the whole power into the hand of the majority of voters in each town or parish, this iniquity has no covering left among us. For ministers are supported by worldly men, who act without any sort of religious qualification, and therefore there is no religion in their doings. And they now violate the most essential rule of all civil governments which is, that the majority of every civil community is the body politic, and that the minority is not the body. Therefore Mr. ELLIS, was never elected as pastor of the first parish in Rehoboth, from whom many thousands of dollars have been taken for him; neither was Mr. Nathan Underwood ever elected the pastor of the second parish in Harwich, by the body of the parish, who have been all taxed to him.

"But Mr. ELLIS'S great success appears to have emboldened Mr. UNDERWOOD, and his collector seized six men who were Baptists, on the first day of December, 1995 [sic], and carried them as far as Yarmouth, where one of them was taken so ill, being old and infirm before, that he saw no way to save his life but to pay the tax and costs, which he did, and the other five were carried to Barnstable prison, where they also paid the money, rather than to lie in a cold prison all winter. And these things moved many to pay said tax, rather than to be strained upon. Tho' as all did not do it, their collector went with aid to the house of one of the Baptists, when he was not at home, Jan. 8, 1796, and seized a cow for a tax to said minister; but his wife and daughter took hold of the cow, and his wife promised to pay the money, if her husband did not, and they let the cow go, and she went to Mr. UNDERWOOD the next day, and paid the tax and costs, and took his receipt therefor.

"Yet 4 days after, the woman and two daughters, one of whom was not there when the cow was taken, were seized and carried before authority, and fined seven dollars for talking to the collector and his aid, and taking hold of the cow while they had her in possession, so that they let her go. These things we have had very distinct accounts of, and if there is the least mistake therein, let them point it out in welcome. Another instance in the County of Plymouth is similar to these in one respect, though not in others. The minister of a Parish lately incorporated, was never chosen by the majority of the inhabitants therein, nor by many who are taxed to him, one of whom was lately seized to be carried to prison, but he paid the money, and others are threatened with like treatment.

"Before this distress was made for the salary of said minister, he got several Baptist ministers to preach in his pulpit, and seems to be in earnest to draw them into compulsive measures also. Yet the line of his parish was extended eight or nine miles from this meeting, in order to take in two valuable lots of ministerial lands, which lie near a Baptist meeting, where a Baptist minister is settled.—These are a few of the evils which have come from the practice of confounding the church and world together, about the government of the church, and the support of religious ministers. Whereas if the civil government would protect all its subjects impartially, without supporting any ministers by tax and compulsion, all true believers would lead a quiet and peaceable life in all godliness and honesty, and the power of other men to oppress them on religious accounts would be taken away."

Brethren—It is not good or safe to chuse a President from out of such a state while such a breach of duty to God and of justice towards men is suffered to dishonor the Government of Massachusetts. —If Evil should hereafter come of it let Pennsylvania keep their conscience clear of the mischief of having called a President from thence. Phocion, an abuser of THOMAS JEFFERSON, insinuates that there was no need of the law introduced by him in Virginia many years ago to repeal all religious impositions and establish liberty of conscience. Ponder all these things in your minds together.

WILLIAM PENN

Commentary on Prayer in Time of War

The General Advertiser (Aurora), March 30, 1798

An author of more than usual merit, after declaring that war is, 'a state in which it becomes our business to hurt and annoy our neighbour by every possible means; instead of cultivating, to destroy; instead of building, to pull down; instead of peopling, to depopulate; a state in which we drink the tears, and feed upon the misery of our fellow creatures;' briefly comments on the methods by which the European governments have contrived to associate it with the religion of Jesus. Their prayers, says this ingenious writer, 'if put into plain language would run thus; God of love, father of all the families of the earth, we are going to tear in pieces our brethren of mankind, but our strength is not equal to our fury, we beseech thee to assist us in the work of slaughter. Go out, we pray thee, with our fleets and our armies; we call them christian, and we have interwoven in our banners, and the decorations of our arms, the symbols of a suffering religion, that we may fight under the cross upon which our saviour died. Whatever mischief we do, we shall do it in thy name; we hope, therefore, thou wilt protect us in it. Thou, who hast made of one blood all the dwellers upon the earth, we trust thou wilt view us alone with partial favour, and enable us to bring misery upon every other quarter of the globe.' Whether supplications, which have ideas similar to these for their genuine import, and which the members of the different hierarchies are so often compelled to utter, are or are not in direct opposition to the benign spirit and the pacific precepts of the gospel, are questions which its most unlettered reader can feel no embarrassment in answering.

Jefferson the Infidel

The Boston Gazette and *Weekly Republican Journal,* August 13, 1798

From *The New-York Daily Gazette*

I have read with pain and indignation the account of a public dinner given to Mr. Jefferson, the Vice-President of the United States, on the Sabbath day, at Fredericksburgh in Virginia.—While I heartily approve of honor being paid to the officers of our government, and reprobate all just and indiscriminate abuse, I think the conduct of Mr. Jefferson and his friends merits severe reprehension. The account which I have seen is accompanied with some remarks, particularly on the impropriety of a high officer countenancing disrespect to the government of his country; immediately too on leaving his seat in the senate, where decisive measures had been taken to oppose an ambitious and rapacious enemy; but what I mean principally to remark is the open and horrid profanation of that day which is holy unto the Lord. It is the first instance of the kind I have ever heard of in this country, and from the time and circumstances must shock every serious mind.

As one of the toasts was "May the press be as free as the circumambient air that we breathe," so the gentleman cannot consequently, blame me for the freedom I now take, at the same time, let them be assured that the press shall never be used, intentional, by me, to propagate sentiments unfavorable to morality and the happiness of mankind. I use it at present to reprove what aims a deadly blow at both these, to hold up their conduct for the execration of my countrymen, and no name, and no consequence shall *deter me from my purpose.* There is a wide difference between misrepresentation and a fair discussion of measures, between calumny and the proof of facts notorious and flagrant. Against the latter there ought to be no bar in a free government. Let "the press be free as the circumambient air."

Why was this dinner made on the Lord's day? Mr. Jefferson arrived on Saturday. Was his business so pressing that he could not stay until Monday? If so, he ought to have travelled on Sunday. It is evident by his staying to partake of the convivial repast that his conscience did not forbid him to travel on that day, and that his business could not be so very pressing. But admitting that it was, then the dinner ought to have been omitted. It was not a work of either necessity or mercy, and consequently a direct violation of the divine commandment.

Was this day chosen in order to show publicly their disregard of it, that they adopted the principles of the French, and joined with them in their impiety? There is too much reason to believe that it was. The sentiments breathed in the toasts are in exact unison with a contempt of the precepts of the Christian religion. There is the more reason to believe that it was the intention, from the known opinions of him for whom the feast was made. And yet one would think a grain of prudence or decency might have taught him that, whatever his speculative notions were, and if even initiated in the society of the Illuminati his conduct would be censured as unbecoming the officer of a Christian nation; that though he regarded not the law of God, yet he ought to regard the law of his country, and enforce it by a good example.

I bless God that the people of America are not yet so far contaminated with the Atheistical principles of the French, as to view the transaction I blame with indifference, or think the Sabbath an unnecessary institution. No, they generally consider it as a moral and wise institution, the observance of which is intimately connected with the peace and order of society, as well as the spiritual and eternal interests of men. Their eyes are more and more opened on this subject by the awful miseries of France, and they deprecate her sins, lest they should partake of her plagues. They esteem the blessing that providence hath given them at this moment a Chief Magistrate who professes the Christian religion, and adorns it by his example. They will be grieved and think it inauspicious to find an opposite behaviour in any in whom they have reposed confidence, especially at this juncture when war is waging not only against the rapine, but the abominable principles of France.

CENSOR MORUM

---

* The Printers in the United States, who wish well to morality, and the prosperity of their country, will please to give a place to the above.

PART 2

Personal Journalism
for a Protestant America

After having successfully fought the Revolutionary War and then the War of 1812 against England, Americans quite naturally assumed that their nation had been blessed by God. From the beginning of the 19th century until well into the 20th century, a spirit of optimism prevailed as Americans set about making of their nation the "shining city on the hill" they believed it was meant to be. But it was an optimism tempered with concern.

In 1812, about 10 million people lived in the United States; by 1850 the population had more than tripled. Where once President John Adams had assumed it would take a thousand years, the steam engine and improved transportation led to an economy based on manufacturing in less than 50. In 1800 there were 15 farmers for every person living in a city; by 1850 the ratio of farmers to urban dwellers had been cut to something like 5.5 to one.

New industries were a magnet for immigrants. In the first wave, many of those new immigrants came from Ireland. To those already in the United States, the Roman Catholic religion the Irish brought with them seemed to be a direct threat to their vision of a Protestant America. But the problem was not just Catholic immigrants. For Protestant churches whose organization and values centered on the kind of community found in small towns, the growing industrial cities represented a source of temptation and licentiousness that would undermine the moral fabric of the nation. And if the cities were bad, the frontier was no better. The Louisiana Purchase opened up vast expanses of land that seemed beyond the reach of civilization.

Seeing the changes in their New Jerusalem brought about by geographic expansion and economic development, the churches responded with recurring calls for revival, religious renewal and reform, first of individuals and then of society. From the Second Great Awakening at the dawn of the 19th century through the 20th century crusades of evangelists such as Dwight Moody, Billy Sunday and then Billy Graham, the emphasis was on saving souls. But just behind that goal was, as theologian/historian Martin Marty points out in his 1984 book, *Pilgrims in their Own Land,* "the dream of one kingdom"—a Protestant America that would be the "shining city on the hill."

In their efforts to create that shining city, the Protestant churches had help from the American press. During the 19th century, newspapers proliferated. National circulation magazines sprang up and became immensely popular sources for information and entertainment. During that period, journalism changed; so, too, did the way the media covered religion. In some ways, journalistic practices were very much like those of the modern era. But in other ways, they held much in common with the ideological journalism of the early years.

When Benjamin Day started the first penny newspaper in New York City in 1833, there were 65 newspapers in the United States with a combined circulation of about 78,000. Thirty years later, there were more than 350 papers having a combined circulation of 1.5 million. Instead of having just a few hundred subscribers, individual papers now counted thousands of readers.

Urbanization and industrialization put large numbers of readers within newspapers' reach, but appealing to the urban masses meant redefining news. Benjamin Day promised readers "all the news of the day." To that mix, James Gordon Bennett's *New York Herald* added local coverage of churches and religious organizations, including the Bible, tract and missionary societies that grew out of the revival and reform movements.

The new mix attracted readers that in turn attracted advertising. That, in turn, gave newspapers the resources to hire staffs of reporters who could actively cover the news. New technologies and better communication and transportation made it possible to send reporters into the field as well as to band together with other newspapers to bring in news from the far reaches of the country in a more timely manner. In spite of Sunday blue laws and over clergy opposition, many papers began publishing on Sunday in response to the growing demand for news during the Civil War.

Until well into the 20th century, publications were individually owned and bore the stamp of their owners. Over the years, journalism became increasingly professionalized; news gradually became separated from opinion. However, journalism remained personal and sometimes polemical.

With most towns of any size having several papers, one paper might be

Whig or Democrat in politics and another Populist. But in religion, most were unabashedly Christian—either because of the convictions of their owner/editors or out of deference to the sensibilities of a majority of their readers. When other religions were covered, it was usually from a mainstream Protestant perspective with mainstream Protestant churches and their allied organizations getting the bulk of the coverage, and both newspapers and magazines unabashedly supporting their causes. By the 1880s some newspapers began setting aside space, most often on Monday, for reports of church meetings and Sunday sermons. By the 1920s, many papers had a church page on Friday or Saturday for coverage of church meetings and announcements of Sunday sermon topics and another one on Monday for reports on sermons from influential churches. By the middle of the 20th century, however, routine coverage of sermons disappeared from most newspapers, leaving Friday and Saturday as the most common days for church pages.

The stories reproduced in the chapters in this section deal with episodes that show how religion helped define American politics and culture from the early 1800s through World War II. Chapter 6 treats the early years of the 19th century when the mainstream Protestantism responded to the challenges of a growing and changing nation with an outpouring of missionary zeal. Chapter 7 provides examples of religion news coverage by James Gordon Bennett, whose work marks the beginning of the transition from religious journalism to religion journalism.

Chapters 8 and 9 illustrate the conflict between the dominant culture and two religious minorities, the Roman Catholics and Latter-day Saints. Chapter 10 includes stories that illustrate religious arguments surrounding the Civil War, while chapters 11 through 14 deal with the recurring calls for revival and reform in the years between the Civil War and World War I. Chapter 11 is devoted to examples drawn from the Rev. Charles Sheldon's attempt to create a mass-circulation Christian newspaper; Chapter 12 deals with revival movements while chapter 13 treats reform efforts more closely allied with the emerging social gospel movement that emphasized reforming society to make it more God-pleasing and thus more conducive to saving souls. That social gospel movement both grew out of and helped promote interest in science and all things scientific; it also represented a split within Protestantism that was at the heart of the Scopes trial, which is the subject of chapter 14.

The stories in chapter 15 represent the end of an era of personal journalism for a Protestant America. They document efforts to cope with disparate and sometimes dissident religious voices in the context of the threat to national security posed by World War II. As such, the stories signal the end of the vision of a Protestant America and the beginning of a more inclusive society.

6

The Missionary Spirit

With the passage of the First Amendment, America officially became a nation without a religion. But instead of spelling doom for religion and religiosity as many had feared, churches responded to the new order by launching what theologian/historian Martin Marty has described as a "soul rush."

At the beginning of the 19th century, evangelists set out to save souls. In the process, they also churched the nation and shaped its culture. As in the First Great Awakening, there were revivals and camp meetings. But the real influence of this Second Great Awakening came from the missionary, tract and Bible societies that sprang up as churches banded together to civilize and Christianize the cities and the frontier. The scope of these new voluntary associations can be seen in an item from the *Harrisburg Chronicle of* June 5, 1826, which reported:

> There are 3000 Bible Societies in the world founded all within twenty years. Their annual receipts are about 1,000,000 ($4,500,000) and more than three millions of Bibles have been distributed over the globe, in 148 different languages.

These new para-church organizations had the support of most newspapers. From the early 1800s on, papers regularly carried stories about them whenever they met. Many of those stories were little more than minutes of meetings; others, like "The Missionary Cause" reproduced in this chapter, capture the fervor of those involved in the cause. That story is a typical example of newspapers' use of contributions from readers to cover the news.

As the writer of that article suggests, foreign missionaries were the heroes. Missionaries in the United States had less prestige, but their efforts to civilize and Christianize those who were "different" influenced politics and shaped the culture.

The editorial, "Our Own Family," concerning missions to the Indians reproduced from *Niles' Register* is somewhat unusual for the period because it suggests that, in the long run, example is more effective than overt efforts at conversion and because it gives respectful voice to a Native American perspective.

Like most Americans of the era, the federal and state governments generally supported missions to the Indians. However, states sometimes kept close watch on missionaries lest they foment Indian uprisings. When that fear led the State of Georgia to charge and then convict Samuel A. Worcester and Elizur Butler for unauthorized missionary activity among the Cherokees, the legal battle over states' rights went all the way to the Supreme Court. The story played out in newspapers around the country.

Beginning on January 12, 1832, the *Vicksburg Advocate and Register* brought the story to Mississippi. Mississippians were, at the time, wrestling with the question of how to deal with the Cherokees who, having been driven from their homes, were passing through Mississippi on their way to the Oklahoma territory. On April 12 and 19, 1832, the Vicksburg paper published the full text of the Supreme Court decision written by Chief Justice John Marshall. Although that decision went against Georgia, the state refused to pardon the missionaries for over 100 years. News of the pardon can be found in the November 11, 1992, *New York Times.*

Efforts to Christianize the slaves raised fears, too, but those efforts also had widespread support. An item in *Niles' Register* on April 21, 1821, documents the kind of laws Southern states frequently passed to prevent such work. At the same time, southern support can be seen in the missionary's letter, reproduced from the *Charleston Mercury.*

The fact that many slaves became Christian gave southerners an excuse for portraying slavery as a benefit. It also spawned efforts, through the Colonization Societies that sprang up around the country, to use those converts to Christianize and civilize Africa. Stories about the Societies appeared in many papers including Rhode Island's *Newport Herald* of March 1, 1787, the *Daily National Intelligencer* of May 25, 1826, and the New Orleans *Daily Picayune* of May 1, 1847. A protest by "free people of color" against the colonization scheme can be found in *Niles' Register* for November 28, 1819.

As Martin Marty points out in his 1984 book, *Pilgrims in Their Own Land,* the goal of the missionaries was "to fill up the American landscape with their own kinds." For the Protestant majority, that meant filling it up with Protestants. Catholics presented the major challenge to that goal; in later years, Mormons were equally suspect. Coverage of the relations between those minority faiths and the Protestant majority is in chapters 8 and 9.

Although Jews suffered less discrimination, they were no more welcome than were other religious minorities. The editorial "Christian Missionaries" from *Niles' Register* illustrates the desire of many to bring the
Jewish minority into the mainstream by making the Jews "one of their own
kind," even as it perpetuates common anti-Jewish stereotypes.

Because of that kind of thinking, New York newspaper publisher M. M.
Noah approached the New York State legislature in January 1820 with a
plan to convert Grand Island in the Niagara River into a safe haven for the
Jews of America. The *Albany Gazette* reported the plan; *Niles' Register*
supported it in a January 29 story. Although the plan went nowhere, the
dream stayed alive for almost 30 years through advocacy in Noah's newspapers, the *New York National Advocate* and later the *Courier & Enquirer,*
and through frequent attacks from his rival, James Gordon Bennett, editor
of the *New York Herald.*

The Missionary Cause

Meeting of the American Board at Portland

New-York Daily Times, September 20, 1851

BOSTON, Saturday, September 13, 1851

MY DEAR R:

While stopping at Boston for a few hours, I comply with your request
to throw together some impressions and general views of the Missionary
Cause, as exhibited at the recent important meeting in Portland, Maine.
Details of what I saw and heard you will not expect me to give, except
so far as these illustrate the general character and aspects of the meeting;
of that a three days' observation of the acts and sayings of the Board,
and some personal acquaintance with their leading men, qualify me to
speak; as to particulars, the papers will be full of them to satiety.

1. *The hold which the Missionary movement now has on the general
mind,* every thoughtful observer must admit on mingling with the great
concourse which has just been gathered from all parts of the Union in
the city of Portland. The American Board is a *National* Society. It is
governed and controlled by a corporate board consisting of 200 gentlemen residing in all the States that have manifested any interest in the

work of Missions. The great West is represented in it, and next year the Society will meet at Cincinnati, Ohio; this week it has met together in the far East, and no more beautiful spot could be found for such a purpose, and none, surely, more hospitable than the well built and prosperous town of Portland. I suppose that five or six thousand persons were added to the population for the time being, and more than 2000 of these were the guests of the citizens during the three days of session; the other thousands went in and out day by day from the country adjacent. There was John Neal opening a Missionary meeting with a short speech, just to start the meeting, as he said; when I last heard this gentlemen he was preaching to New-Yorkers in the Tabernacle, 12 years since, "a new Gospel," upon the words "Him whom you ignorantly worship, Him declare I unto you"—the introduction to a Lecture on gymnastic training; and there stood up an excellent Missionary who had lived for 30 years among the Choctaws,—he thought it very strange that people should ask him so often, if the Choctaws were *civilized*; they paid their debts, without making long talks about it, and at one stroke had appropriated $24,000 annually, for twenty years, to the support of common schools—this was done just after receiving a government annuity; besides, had not the Choctaws utterly prohibited the sale of intoxicating liquors, by laws as stringent and summary as those of Maine herself? All classes and descriptions of men were represented in this convocation. Lawyers, judges and chancellors; generals, merchants and mechanics; doctors of medicine and of divinity; sailors and seamens' chaplains; makers of books, farmers and college professors; and of noble and notable women not a few. Is there any middling class in this country of sovereigns?

If it were constitutional to affirm its existence, I should say that the body of the great assemblies gathered at Portland belonged to the very best portion of this class, intelligent-looking, well dressed, well-mannered men and women, the salt of New-England, in numbers sufficient to fill those large churches.

The tone and complexion of the debates showed that it is becoming more and more a settled thing that this Missionary movement must go on to its consummation. It is well known that this state of things has been brought about in part by great dilligence in spreading the facts of the case before the public; these distinct publications have been issued during the year, with an average monthly circulation of 18,000, 41,000 and 55,000, respectively. Men in every department of life expressed with much earnestness of feeling their determination to give this cause a large place in their business plan. One of your New-York lawyers, besides largely increasing his individual contributions, means to keep a book in his office, labelled "American Board," and intends asking everybody that steps in to put down something; his friends must look out for this gentle-man.

2. *Confidence in the official management of the Board* was strongly marked at the meeting. The executive power of the Society resides at Boston, consisting of a Prudential Committee, and three Secretaries for correspondence. The reputation of these gentlemen for successful man-agement of the affairs committed to them, stands very high in the com-mercial world; no business house has better credit or sustains a fairer name. The sum of $300,000 is annually collected by their agents in this country, and disbursed at their missionary stations throughout the world.

3. *The character of our Missionaries,* as men of rare qualifications, and of rare success in their labors, is matter of commendation on all hands. There could hardly be higher or more valuable testimony on this score than a remark of the late distinguished Dr. Arnold who spoke of the American Missionaries in the Mediterranean and elsewhere, as by all accounts surpassing those of other nations, and of our country as going far before Great Britain in this enterprise, to *their* great reproach, he added.

They are unquestionably, as a class, men of intellectual vigor and of power; they have the strength, akin to the inspirations of genius, which comes from whole-souled devotion to a great cause. I have never heard better speaking, in the true elements of persuasive discourse, than the earnest speeches of some of these gentlemen, straight from the heart. The Missionary, Spaulding, of Ceylon, had a remarkable power of giving a picture by a word; when I heard him on his last visit to this country, he seemed, as he began to speak, to have but "few words of English speech;" but the right word always came at the right moment, and every word weighed a pound—it shone clear and and [sic] bright, like a coin fresh from the mint. Mr. Goodell, for thirty years resident at Constan-tinople, made repreated addresses at the late meeting, racy and spirit-stir-ring; a quaint, strange diction, the language of patriarchs and prophets come to life again. Full of strong, deep feeling was the soul of the excel-lent Byington, from Stockbridge, Mass., but during 31 years a Mission-ary among the Choctaws. The experiment of civilizing the Indians has succeeded well in the instance of that nation; there is no need, apparently, of their wasting away before the advance of civilization, as has been often asserted respecting those tribes. The Choctaws desire education, and they are now providing it for themselves; more than 1,200 of them are Church members, and in their country just laws are strictly and impartially enforced.

Yesterday morning we listened to the farewell speeches of several Missionaries. One would not say farewell; he told us he was not going far, and soon we should meet again. You are employed about the same work, he told us; occupied in the same field with us; while busy on your farms, at your merchandise, in every part of this country, we are all laborers together, and my word to you is, "ALL HAIL!" This salutation of Mr. Walker, Missionary at Gaboon, Western Africa, was a cheering and reviving word. Rev. Mr. Wood, of Constantinople, expressed briefly and happily his deep thankfulness at the welcome he had found in so many homes and hearts during his recent visit to America; and the joy he felt in the prospect of soon returning to his work abroad, where he had spent the happiest years of his life.

Missionaries gave great interest to this anniversary meeting. At two or three different times they assembled together with their families and friends—those who have returned and those, also, who are soon to go forth for the first time. On these occasions one would rise and another, from Africa, Asia and the Islands; and with a simple expression of pious feeling, or by a brief narrative of events, make himself known to the brethren of the several missions, or throw out some valuable thoughts for those that stay at home. These were among the most delightful reunions; men from various countries, and, in fact, representatives of the Church as existing among many different nations, all here speaking one language and declaring the wonderful works of God. Of those Missionaries, their families and immediate relations, there were present perhaps 100 persons.

With regard to the extent of the Society's operations, the work already done and their future promise, I must cut short my account, or I could name a multitude of interesting particulars.

Nearly four hundred missionaries, sent out from the United States, are now in the service of this Society; and in the churches which they have organized there are twenty-four thousand communicants. Africa has forty of these missionaries, and from their posts on the western and southern coasts of the continent, they are endeavoring to penetrate the interior, which thus far has been unexplored. At Athens, Greece, Dr. King fires away at the superstitions and vices of modern Athenians. In

Western Asia, a spiritual reformation has made cheering progress; and this formed the subject of earnest discussion at the recent meeting. Dr. Beman, of Troy, read a strong paper respecting the *Armenian* (not the *"American,"* as some newspapers have it), Reformation, and the encouragement afforded by it to increased labor in that most interesting country. To that region, the cradle of the human race, Americans are now bearing back the light of a pure gospel. Professor Thobeck, of Germany, says that he looks upon none of our labors with so much interest as upon those which are now bestowed upon the Western Asiatic nations, the centre of the World. To the Protestants in that nation the Sultan has recently granted an ample charter, conferring on them all the privileges possessed by his other subjects. The privileges guaranteed by this instrument are now enjoyed by 1500 Protestants.

A Mission has been established at Mosul Assyria, near which are the remarkable ruins of ancient Ninevah. Among the mountains of Persia, forty-five schools have been established for the instruction of Nestorian children and youth, and the missionaries are encouraged to hope for the conversion of this entire people.

In India, five Missions are maintained, with their complement of schools, seminaries and churches. At the Sandwich Islands hardly a man of the native population is now unable to read and write, and during the last year, $43,000 were expended upon schools, $32,000 of which were the gift of the Government. Far beyond these islands the missionaries are now urging their way, and very soon a company will proceed on an exploring expedition west and south, with the design to plant teachers and preachers on those distant groups.

At the beginning of the meeting the Society was in debt to the amount of $44,000; at the close of the meeting pledges had been received covering nearly half of this sum. A good meeting has been held, deepening and extending the interest felt by thousands of churches, and hundreds of thousands of believers in the missionary cause.   M.

Our Own Family

Niles' Register, April 14, 1821

"He that does not provide for his own family is worse than an infidel." The truth of this saying comes directly to the senses and he must be a bad member of society, indeed, who does not feel and acknowledge it.

While our country is inundated with societies, based on the best affections of the heart and aiming at the most sublime results to do good to *foreigners*—to send our missions to the *East Indies,** to disseminate the scriptures in the South-sea islands, &c—when we are infested with wretches playing on our charity for the relief of christian slaves in Algiers to repair damages occasioned by an overflowing of the Rhine,† and build churches, for what I know, on the eternally snow capt summit of Caucasus, &c—while we feel ready to give money to relieve the distresses of those lately burnt out in the *moon,* by the bursting of a volcano recently discovered therein, provided a good story could be told us *as how* the news of such distress could be received here, and *as how* the offerings of our credulity [the gifts of lunarians to *the* Lunarians] were to be transmitted there,—the following brief account of the progress of improvement among the Cherokee Indians, must afford great pleasure to the really charitable heart. It is not the business of these worthy people, who have taken up their abode in the wilderness, to "spy out the nakedness of the land" and point the path by which the destroyer shall advance on his prey: but, influenced by the spirit of truth, they TEACH the gospel instead of *preaching* it, and exhibit its benefits in a harmless life devoted to good works—inviting the poor Indian to civilization, as the only means of preserving his race from annihilation, and of preparing him for an adoption into the great American family, on an equal footing with his white brethren, in due season. These excellent people are quietly proceeding in their work: content in their honest endeavors and regardless of fame; and appear to have "began their business at the right end." Their schools have long been highly spoken of, and the proof of the advantages of them is in the fact, that the Cherokees (resident east of the Mississippi) are remarkable for civil improvement and domestic virtue.

It has always been our earnest desire that some, even one, of the Indian tribes should be won to an incorporation with the nation, for the sake of humanity—for the honor of our country. We know that there is an honest zeal existing to ameliorate their condition and confer upon them some of the advantages of civilization, to lessen the misery which the approaches of a white population heaps upon them—that such is the desire of the government and earnest wish of thousands of philanthropic individuals, but the wishes and the labors of both have been generally defeated by the intrigues and crimes of base men seeking an unfair and destructive trade with the Indians, to supply them with rum in exchange

for their skins and lands—to keep them in the hunter-state, though that
evidently leads to their utter extinction—if in the vicinity of settlements
of white people: but we want something, one solitary fact to point at,
that will "tell well in history," and shew the sincerity of our endeavors to
do good to this injured people. Their habits and manners, it must be admitted, renders the task exceedingly difficult—they cannot brook dicta-
tion or restraint, and must be delicately dealt with. Long accustomed to
regard white men as intruders upon them, and generally subjected to additional sufferings and privations as our settlements extend,—oftentimes
cheated and basely deceived, it is difficult for them to apprehend that
any person really comes among them disinterestedly, for their good: and
this is not to be wondered at, seeing that we find so few persons among
ourselves that are truly capable of giving up their private interests to a
performance of the virtues. Self-interest is our leading star, and even on
the very brink of the grave, we see that many are grasping at the goods
of this world. Those then, who are permitted to reside among the Indians
with a view to their improvement, should be of humble spirits, patient
and forbearing—*working* persons, as farmers, smiths, carpenters, &c.
thus making themselves useful and productive; not consumers of the
scanty supplies of the inhabitants of the woods.‡ The axe and the plough,
the hammer and the saw, should precede preaching, and in handling
these the means of comfort which the Great Spirit affords, will be better
illustrated to the Indians, than by the most learned dissertations on texts
of scripture. Some attempts have been made in this way by the Quakers,
and at Wapakanetta and other places, which have measurably succeeeded, though much interrupted by intruding whites, who lead the Indians astray. The establishment of schools [i]s of the highest importance—not schools to learn reading and writing only, but to lead the
boys to a love of farming, smithing, &c. and the girls to spinning, knit-
ting, sewing, &c. which we understand is the practice at Wapakanetta,
Brainard, &c. If a regard for these things can be established in their
minds, and they once feel the advantages that result, from a practice of
them, all else that is needful will naturally follow.

*Extract of a letter from a gentleman, one of the mission family at
Brainard, in the Cherokee nation, to his friend in the city of New London, dated January 18, 1821.*

"Our school continues to prosper—we have between eighty and
ninety fine children—they are improving as fast as could be expected—

there is an increasing desire among the natives to have their children educated—the nation is rapidly increasing in civilization—at their last
council they divided their country into eight districts, appointed circuit
judges, sheriffs, constables and justices, and laid a tax on the people to
build a court house in each district. They begin to pay very considerable
attention to cultivating their land—there are many good persons among
them.

It no longer remains a doubt whether the Indians of America can be
civilized—the Cherokees have gone too far in the pleasant path of civilization to return to the rough and unbeaten track of savage life."

----

*The *bible* is too often used in the East Indies as the precursor of the sword. It
has more or less been the practice of all the nations who have had much to do with
the desolation of India, to send our priests as spies—the word of life on their lips and
the dagger concealed in their bosoms! I recollect to have seen a letter from some
canting scoundrel, who, after relating the kind manner in which he had been treated
by the Indians, how attentively they listened to his discourses, &c. concluded with a
description of the riches of the country, saying it furnished "a fine field for his
majesty's arms!"—that is, his Britannic majesty's. The British in India have been the
immediate cause of the death of not less than fifty millions of the human race in fifty
years; and a sense of this destruction probably led to the determination of one of the
native princes, as thus given in a Calcutta paper of the 14th of July last.—

"The missionaries at Rangoon, repaired to the capital on the accession of the present monarch, in order to congratulate him and solicit his protection; when he returned for answer that they might freely profess their own religion within his territories and preach as they pleased; but if any Birmans quitted the religion of the country
to join them, he would decapitate the apostates."

†In the 19th, or last volume of the REGISTER, page 210, we inserted a notice
from the mayor of Philadelphia, of the discovery of a nest of wretches who, under
pretence of redeeming captives in Algiers, building churches, &c. were swindling the
people out of their money, as charitable gifts for such purposes. They were well furnished with various documents of their own manufacture. One of this nest, or at least
a fellow engaged in the same business, has been caught in Indiana. He had a great
variety of documents *in blank,* to fill up at his discretion, as he chose to assume a
new character, and about three thousand dollars in good money! He was permitted to
pass after destroying his documents and papers, and compelling him to return the
money which he had collected in the neighborhood.

‡The famous Seneca chief, *Red Jacket,* lately sent a letter, or talk, to governor
Clinton, of New-York, complaining of many trespasses upon the Indians. Among
other things he says—

"Our great father, the president, has recommended to our young men to be industrious, to plough and to sow. This we have done, and we are thankful for the advice,

and for the means he has afforded us of carrying it into effect.—We are happier in consequence of it. But another thing recommended to us, has created great confusion among us, and is making us a quarrelsome and divided people; and that is the introduction of preachers into our nation. These black coats contrive to get the consent of some of the Indians to preach among us: and whenever this is the case, confusion and disorder are sure to follow; and the encroachments of the whites upon our lands, are the invariable consequence. The governor must not think hard of me speaking thus of the preachers. I have observed their progress, and when I look back to see what has taken place of old, I preceive that whenever they came among the Indians, they were the forerunners of their dispersion, that they always excited enmities and quarrels among them; that they introduced the white people on their lands, by whom they were robbed and plundered of their property; and that the Indians were sure to dwindle and decrease, and be driven back, in proportion to the number of preachers that came among them.

"Each nation has its own customs, and its own religion. The Indians have theirs, given to them by the Great Spirit, under which they were happy.—It was not intended that they should embrace the religion of the whites, and be destroyed by the attempt to make them think differently on that subject, from their fathers.

"It is true, these preachers have got the consent of some of the chiefs, to stay and to preach among us; but I and my friends know this to be wrong, and that they ought to be removed. Besides, we have been threatened by Mr. Hyde, who came among us as school-master, and a teacher of our children, but has now become a black coat, and refuses to them any more, that unless we listen to his preaching, and become christians, we will be turned off our lands, and not allowed to plague us any more; we shall never be at peace while he is among us.

"We are afraid too, that these preachers, by and by, will become poor, and force us to pay them for living among us."

Mission to the Slaves

Charleston Mercury, August 28, 1860

To the Editor of the Mercury:

From the would-be friends of the colored people, whose philanthropy is of the most suspicious and dangerous character, and whose interference has done those people a great injury, it is pleasant to turn to the kind attention of the many Christian masters, whose philanthropy is of a very different kind, not in words (as the prating of Abolitionists), but in deeds of kindness, both physical and spiritual, to the people whom Providence has placed under their particular care. And it is refreshing, to know that the people, many of them feel that their masters are their very best friends. I was especially impressed with this idea on last Sunday, while attending to my duties on the Mission in St. John's Parish. My plan has been, when we have implicit confidence in a member of the church, and whose piety is not doubted, to occasionally call upon such a one to close the services by prayer, as my labors on the Sabbath are generally severe, as was the case on last Sunday, having to preach four times, administer the Sacrament twice, and baptize some seven persons, and ride serveral miles in attending the appointment. Several of the owners of the plantations I visited being absent, travelling for their health, the burden of the prayers was for the safe return of their masters and for their families. If some of those persons who are so loud in their opposition to the institution, could see the affection existing between the owners and their slaves, especially between the nurses and the children (that word *mauma* comes so sweetly from the little one's lips), they would soon change their opinion, I think, if they are not so completely prejudiced as not to believe their own eyes.

Those missions to the slaves are accomplishing more than I fear some of the planters are willing to acknowledge. My own opinion, which is based on an experience of many years in this particular field of labor, is that the leaven of the Gospel seed sown in their hearts is working silently, but surely; and I think our congregations, for good order and propriety, can compare very favorably with any others, either in the city or country. It does seem to me that the true interest of the masters should be to encourage this good work among their people, by putting up proper buildings for the worship of God, and by contributing more liberally to the support of those missions, and occasionally to be present (as some have done) and worship with their people, to encourage them. While the Southern people are liberal in giving of their means to Foreign Missions, they should be more liberal in their contributions to Home Missions.

A MISSIONARY.

Christian Missionaries

Niles' Register, November 13, 1819

Many well disposed persons, in most parts of the Christian world, are deeply exercised to spread the light and benefit of the gospel to the uttermost parts of the earth, and give their time and money freely for the support of missions and missionaries; and, in respect to some of the latter, though we do not approve of their general manner of proceeding, it is impossible to withold our admiration of the patience and perseverence with which they meet and sustain themselves under the multitudinous hardships and privations to which they are liable.

Without reference to any particular case, we apprehend that the work of conversion is commonly *began at the wrong end.* The Christian dispensation, unpolluted by religious factionists, is, of all others *infinitely* best calculated for the government of man in the highest possible state of improvement that mortals can aspire to; and, as improvement advances and society becomes polished, the *necessity* of obedience to its leading precepts becomes more and more manifest. Without a feeling of this necessity, the labors of the missionaries among the heathen must continue to be profitless. Missions also are too often bottomed on political views—and the converts, instead of being "set free" by the gospel, are made slaves by the sword—in other cases, they are vexed by *parties,* and rather become worshippers of men than of God.

If it is desired that a people shall be converted to Christianity, let them be prepared by teaching them the use of the plough and the hammer—by instructing them in the agricultural and mechanic arts, through the agency of discreet workmen, who may practically shew them the benefits of industry, temperance, forbearance, &c. with a reverence for the Giver of all good gifts, as the base of our religion. If these proferred advantages are embraced, the teachers of righteousness may expect to reap a bountiful harvest. But it ought to be considered as high treason against common sense, for any one to deal in the dogmas of his sect—to extol one *mode* of worship and condemn another. The really pious man may do all that is appointed to him, without introducing the confusion of faction into the mind of his disciple, where all should be harmony. A *partizan* preacher should not be suffered any more go out as a missionary to teach the gospel to the heathen, than a tyger be sent to them as emblematic of mercy.

These brief remarks occurred by seeing in the newspapers an account of a "converted Jew," who is travelling through the Russian dominions, under the patronage of the emperor, to distribute Hebrew Testaments and religious tracts among the Jewish people, who are very numerous in some parts of the empire; and we have thought that, even as to the Jews themselves, the emperor would be most apt to succeed in the design of making Christians of them, if he were first to convert them into agriculturalists and mechanics, which it is within his power to do. This people have been so much and so long persecuted by pretended Christians, that they do not seem to have a *home* any where; and hence, in our opinion, it is, that so few of them are manual laborers. They are nearly all of them money-changers or dealers—and multitudes of them are continually travelling from place to place, buying and selling. Perhaps, not one in a hundred of them *produces* any thing useful by his own hands. We never knew of one that regularly *worked* for his living. It is not in the nature of man to act thus, nor is it the condition on which society exists—but this sect has been thrown into the *unproductive* class by oppression; and their religion itself is doubly endeared to them by the persecutions which they suffer on account of it. If they were treated like *men*—no one can hesitate to believe that in a few generations they would assimilate with, and, for all useful purposes become *national* in the countries wherein they might be located; and fall into the common manners and habits of the society in which they resided.

Had Napoleon Bonaparte restrained himself so as to have kept possession of the throne of France, no event, perhaps, would have marked his reign more strongly than a regeneration of the Jews—i.e, from wandering tribes of pedlars, or stationary money-changers and traffickers, he would have converted them into *Frenchmen*—by the powerful liberality which he extended towards them.

7

The Birth of Modern Religion Reporting

Although historians such as Michael Schudson have characterized James Gordon Bennett as "a man of little religious feeling," it was Bennett who captured for history the religious fervor of early 19th-century America. In the process, he forever changed the way newspapers approached religion. Where earlier newspapers had provided a kind of "religious journalism," Bennett introduced "religion journalism."

Newspapers had always covered religion, but their coverage consisted primarily of letters and essays written from an insider's perspective to defend or promote a particular religion. In contrast, Bennett wrote from the perspective of an outside observer. His religion coverage emphasized behavior, not beliefs. Bennett rarely used the Bible to argue the correctness of one religious belief over another. He did, however, use both examples from the ministry of Jesus and the U.S. Constitution to scrutinize beliefs and behaviors for their consequences on individuals and on society.

Although much has been made of the irreverent, satirical and sometimes sensational tone of much of the news in the early *New York Herald,* much of that came from Bennett's fascination with and coverage of religious hypocrisy and the interconnections among religion, money, politics and power. In covering those subjects, Bennett paved the way for hard news coverage and investigative reporting about religion. However, his work also provided the model for the traditional church page with its emphasis on church histories, religious events, worship services and individual examples of charitable and moral behavior.

In the *Herald* there were tasteless and tacky fillers, satires, more serious editorials and commentaries, straight news and news analyses. The stories reproduced in this chapter illustrate the kinds of coverage of religion for which Bennett became both famous and infamous. Other examples that illustrate Bennett's concern for religious liberty and for the rights of religious minorities can be found in chapters 8 and 9.

Although he published only two excerpts from what he admitted was a work of fiction, the first excerpt from the "Awful Disclosures by Maria Monk" illustrates the kind of sensational attention to religion that made

Bennett infamous and that, over time, led clergy, business leaders and rival editors to foment a Moral War against him. However, in spite of the criticism he received, Bennett never shied away from covering real news of sexual improprieties on the part of the clergy. One of the more noteworthy examples is the August 1, 1844, publication of court testimony from the Rev. Joy Fairchield, who was on trial for having an affair with one of his parishioners.

"Holy Evergreens" is an example of Bennett at his satirical best. That satire also illustrates his fascination with the corrupting power of money. The reference to Anneke Jants both alludes to earlier coverage of Trinity Episcopal Church's claim to her estate at the expense of her family and foreshadows subsequent attention to Trinity's vast wealth and political influence.

"Religion and Salvation" is Bennett's classic defense of his own independent and somewhat idiosyncratic allegiance to Roman Catholicism. In the words "judge . . . what their acts may justify," Bennett provides the clearest and most succinct summary of his approach to religion reporting.

Although Bennett made his name first by providing sensational and satirical attention to religion, one of his most lasting contributions to the field of religion reporting came from his serious and systematic attention to the annual meetings and activities of both major denominations and the para-church organizations that sprang up during the Second Great Awakening.

The story about the Bible Society that is included in this chapter is very short by Bennett's standards. However, in other respects it is typical of the many stories of annual meetings published in the *Herald* each May and June. Like those longer stories, it is a blend of the scene-setting description and detailed, factual reporting that made Bennett's reporting so appealing to a mass audience.

Initially Bennett wrote most of the news himself, but as his paper prospered, he was able to hire reporters to cover simultaneously occurring local events and bring him news from around the country. "Religious Intelligence" is an early example of the roundup column that subsequently became a staple on and off the church page. As in the Bible Society story, the imbedded commentary provides hints of Bennett's interest in the interplay between religion and politics.

"A Revival in Saratoga Springs" once again documents the mixture of piety and hypocrisy that Bennett found in most religions. In that story, the correspondent employs Bennett's writing style to create a rather unflatter-

ing but probably relatively accurate description of one of the many revivals that were a regular feature of religious life in the years after the Second Great Awakening.

From "Awful Disclosures by Maria Monk"

New York Herald, January 19, 1836

*Taking the Veil.—Interview afterwards with
the Superior.—Surprise and Horror at the
Disclosures.—Resolution to Submit*

I was introduced into the Superior's room in the evening preceding
the day on which I was to take the veil, to have an interview with the
Bishop. The Superior was present, and the interview lasted about half an
hour. The bishop, on this as on other occasions, appeared to me habitually rough in his manners. His address was by no means prepossessing.

Before I took the veil, I was ornamented for the ceremony, and was
clothed in a rich dress belonging to the convent, which was used on such
occasions; and placed not far from the altar in the chapel, in the view of
a number of spectators, who had assembled, in number, perhaps about
forty. Taking the veil is an affair which occurs so frequently in Montreal,
that it has long ceased to be regarded as a novelty; and, although notice
had been given in the French parish church as usual, only a small audience had assembled, as I have mentioned.

Being well prepared with a long training, and frequent rehearsals, for
what I was to perform, I stood waiting in my large flowing dress, for the
appearance of the Bishop. He soon presented himself, entering by the
door behind the altar; I then threw myself at his feet, and asked him to
confer upon me the veil. He expressed his consent; and then, turning to
the Superior, I threw myself prostrate at her feet, according to my instructions, repeating what I had before done at rehearsals, and made a
movement as if to kiss her feet. This she prevented, or appeared to prevent, catching me by a sudden motion of her hand and granted my request. I then kneeled before the Holy Sacrament, that is, a large round
wafer held by the Bishop between his fore-finger and thumb, and made
my vows.

This wafer I had been taught to regard with the utmost veneration, as the real body of Jesus Christ, the presence of which made the vows uttered before it binding in the most solemn manner.

After taking the vows, I proceeded to a small apartment behind the altar, accompanied by four nuns, where was a coffin prepared, with my nun name engraved upon it:—

"SAINT EUSTACE."

My companions lifted it by four handles attached to it, while I threw off my dress, and put on that of a nun of Soeur Bourgeoise; and then we all returned to the chapel. I proceeded first, and was followed by the four nuns; the Bishop naming a number of worldly pleasures in rapid succession, in reply to which I as rapidly repeated—"Je renonce, Je renonce, Je renonce,"—[I renounce, I renounce, I renounce.] [Translation in original.]

The coffin was then placed in front of the altar, and I advanced to place myself in it. This coffin was to be deposited, after the ceremony, in an out-house, to be preserved until my death, when it was to receive my corpse. There were reflections which I naturally made at that time, but I stepped in, extended myself, and lay still. A pillow had been placed at the head of the coffin, to support my head in a comfortable position. A large, thick, black cloth was then spread over me, and the chanting of Latin hymns immediately commenced. My thoughts were not the most pleasing during the time I lay in that situation. The pall, or Drap Mortel, as the cloth is called, had a strong smell of incense which was always disagreeable to me, and then proved almost suffocating. I recollected also a story I had heard of a novice, who, in taking the veil, lay down in her coffin like me, and was covered in the same manner, but on the removal of the covering was found dead. When I was uncovered I rose, stepped out of my coffin, and kneeled. Other ceremonies then followed, of no particular interest; after which, the music commenced, and here the whole was finished.—I then proceeded from the chapel, and returned to the Superior's room, followed by the other nuns, who walked two by two, in their customary manner, with their hands folded on their breasts, and their eyes cast down upon the floor. The nun who was to be my companion in future, then walked at the end of the procession. On reaching the Superior's door, they all left me, and I entered alone, and found her with the Bishop and two priests.

The Superior now informed me, that having taken the black veil, it only remained that I should swear the three oaths customary on becoming a nun; and that some Explanation would be necessary from her. I was now, she told me, to have access to every part of the edifice, even to the cellar, where two of the sisters were imprisoned for causes which she did not mention, I must be informed that one of my great duties was to obey the priests in all things; and this I soon learned, to my utter astonishment and horror, was to live in the practice of criminal intercourse with them. I expressed some of the feelings which this announcement excited in me, which came upon me like a flash of lightning; but the only effect was to set her arguing with me, in favor of the crime, representing it as a virtue acceptable to God, and honorable to me. The priests, she said, were not situated like other men, being forbidden to marry; while they lived secluded, laborious, and self-denying lives, for our salvation. They might, indeed, be considered our saviours, as without their services we could not obtain pardon of sin, and must go to hell. Now it was our solemn duty, on withdrawing from the world, to consecrate our lives to religion, to practice every species of self-denial. We could not become too humble, nor mortify our feelings too far; this was to be done by opposing them, and acting contrary to them; and what she proposed was, therefore, pleasing in the sight of God. I now felt how foolish I had been to place myself in the power of such persons as were around me.

From what she said I could draw no other conclusion, but that I was required to act like the most abandoned of beings, and that all my future associates were habitually guilty of the most heinous and detestable crimes. When I repeated my expressions of surprise and horror, she told me that such feelings were very common at first, and that many other nuns had expressed themselves as I did, who had long since changed their minds. She even said that on her entrance into the nunnery, she had felt like me.

[To be continued.]

Holy Evergreens

New York Herald, December 14, 1836

MR. BENNETT

Do not you think that the amount of money expended for Christmas Greens to dress up Churches with, could be better laid out? There are between twenty and thirty Episcopal Churches in the city, that pay from five to fifteen dollars each for evergreens. Now if this money were paid for fuel or clothing for the poor, how much relief it would give! If you get this done, you will be the poor man's friend.

HARRIETTE SMITH.

ANSWER.—I doubt, my dear Miss Harriette, whether I can be a poor man's friend in this case. The property of the Episcopal Church in this city is immense, and it will continue to be immense till the descendents of Anneka Jants get their own. It is utterly impossible to get rid of the property, or to bring the revenue within the limits of law, unless we expend it in every way that can be devised.

The purchase of beautiful evergreens at the very highest prices, not only helps to get rid of this surplus revenue of the Church, but it also circulates money during the present pressure, and furnishes, besides, a very fine relief to the eye when you enter church, to say your matins or sing your vespers—*Sancte Maria*—or otherwise thank Heaven that the Court of Errors (blessed be their errors) have not yet decided against you. It is true, the poor might be much aided by a few hundred dollars, as suggested by kindly Harriette Smith, but Eliza, her sister, says that the poor are so much accustomed to hunger and want, that pinching is necessary for their health and spirit at this season of the year.

Be that as it may, I do love to see God's holy churches look cheerful and evergreen on Christmas and New Year's days. It is a picture of the beauty and verdure of religion. If we might be permitted to imagine how the spirits of the just decorate Heaven on Christmas day, we would array its thrones, altars, columns of gold and pyramids of alabaster, with the freshest and purest evergreens taken from the trees of Paradise, where they are spreading freshness and fragrance along the banks of the clear stream of Eden eastward. If Trinity Church, or St. Pauls, or St. Thomas, or all the other Saintly Churches in the Episcopal calendar, are not beautifully and elegantly decorated, we shall give them one of the severest paragraphs they ever had. They ought to rejoice, if for nothing else, that they are still enjoying the vast property of Anneke Jants, and that many of her children's children are wandering pennyless around the Union as very useful examples to teach patience and resignation under misfortune and the law's delay, as well as give a lively example of sagacity of churchmen in holding on to what they get with a miser's grasp.

Let the best evergreens be got that Long Island can afford. The poor we have always with us—cheap and plenty. We must get rid of the church surplus in some way. It is as troublesome as Gen. Jackson's. We must be religious, elegant, expensive, and even buy evergreens for Churches! Why not decorate every parlor in which company is received on New Year's day with wreaths of evergreens? How beautiful a beautiful woman looks, surrounded with fragrant evergreens! Let it be done.

Religion and Salvation

New York Herald, December 14, 1838

I have received several letters, begging me to turn my attention to the state of my soul, expressing an opinion that my salvation is in a precarious condition, and entreating me to bestow a little time on the merits of the Episcopalians, if I could be induced to change my ancient faith for a modern. It is also mentioned that Dr. Wainwright of St. John's, Dr. Hawks of St. Thomas', or Dr. Schroeder, of St. Paul's, would be able to set my mind right in true religious opinions.

I have often thought of this subject, and have heard Dr. Wainwright with some pleasure, but little or no profit. In the Doctor's preaching it always appeared to me that he did not heartily believe in the doctrines he put forth. In matters of faith, I am an enthusiast. I believe in the Virgin and all that belongs to her—and if such an intelligent clergyman as Dr. Wainwright does not equally believe in those delicious and charming mysteries, I can only set him down as an infidel to the holy petticoat, and all that it contains. Religion—true religion—consists not in eating or drinking—not in high salaries—not in hanging round the apron strings of rich old women—not in presuming to judge the opinions of others beyond what their acts will justify. Neither does true religion—or real Christianity consist in believing the dogmas of any church—or the *ipse dixit* of any set of men. The Bible is before me. Have I not a right to read that book—to draw out from it religious opinions—and to create a belief and a church of my own? Perhaps Dr. Wainwright may think that the Trinity Church Corporation ought to have a monopoly of religion and roast beef, as it has of certain vast estates, which belong to other individuals.

On the whole, I begin to think, from what I hear of the clergy of the Episcopal Church, of their recent "sayings and doings"—that a gradual and thorough reform is wanted in that quarter. Their immense estates have created a similar state of morals which have characterized the locofocos and sub-treasury men. More of this by and by. Surplus revenue of any kind, is a dangerous thing.

Bible Society Anniversary

New York Herald, May 23, 1836

Bright and beautiful did the sun rise yesterday morning. The sky was pure—the air serene—and all over New York—the fragrance breathed as if it had just been imported direct from Paradise. Our numerous religious strangers rose early and said their prayers just loud enough to be heard on high. The youth and beauty of the city began to stir at nine o'clock. The pious, the philanthropic, the wise, the Christian all started together, and by ten minutes past ten, one of the most splendid congregations had assembled in the great Tabernacle that ever graced that magnificient habitation of the holy.

It was the Anniversary of the Bible Society.

The Bible—what can we say of that book? It has revolutionised the world. It yet contains the seeds of a thousand conflicts with Satan and two thousands of religious intellectual movements in society. Talk to us indeed of Homer's Poems—of the Sybilian Leaves—of the Institutions of Menu! Were the Scriptures but a human production, they have already produced more effect on the human race than all the other works in the world.

The Tabernacle was full from top to bottom—from floor to ceiling. Parsons, preachers, widows, old, young, single, married, sinners, saints, all mingled together in one mass—piled up on each other like bundles of blessedness in the granneries of Paradise. Behind the pulpit, which rises in the centre like the glory of another Cherubim, were seated, file by file, the whole host of stranger clergymen who are now wandering through our city spelling the signs and inquiring for the scene of Ellen Jewett's awful murder. Elsewhere nothing was to be seen but bonnets, feathers, ostriches plumes, birds of paradise, and towering head dresses. Possibly lovely female faces were under these canopies, but as to that we cannot positively swear to.

Mr. Dunlap of Maine was speaking. He was formerly a politician of our school—the Jackson school—now he is a saint. Jackson politics always end in a spirit of devotion. Like the celebrated age of Louis XIV, politics lead to devotion—so does a member of the Kitchen become always the best saint of the day. Mr. Dunlap was eloquent and powerful. He pictured forth in high colors the beauties of the Bible. He exhibited its effects on society—he carried conviction to all. The meeting was also addressed by half a dozen Reverends from various parts of the country, and wound up with a spirited speech from Peter A. Jay. During the last year $45,000 were appropriated to the dissemination of the Scriptures in the following way:

English Bibles,	63,160
English Testaments,	150,018
German Bibles,	1,996
German Testaments,	1,818
French Bibles,	593
French Testaments,	756
Spanish Bibles,	169
Spanish Testaments,	213
Modern Greek Testaments,	3,646
Portuguese Bibles and Testaments,	51
Welsh Bibles and Testaments,	66
Arabic, Syriac, Swedish and Dutch Bibles and Testaments,	56
Italian, Polish, Danish, Gaelic and Indian,	73

Making in all, 221,694 copies, and an aggregate since the formation of the society of 1,989,430.

Religious Intelligence

New York Herald, July 27, 1840

The Rev. Mr. Beatty of the Dutch Reformed Church, late of New Utrecht, Long Island, is about establishing a church in Buffalo. He is a gentleman of great erudition and piety, and as a logician and sound preacher is not surpassed, and we believe not equalled by any other clergyman of that persuasion in this country. We have this information from a gentleman of high standing in New Utrecht, and who is thoroughly competent to judge. We wish his undertaking every success.

The Rev. Dr. Cox, in a series of communications called the "Hexagon," (six doctrinal points,) is handling the Old School Calvinists without mercy. The doctor is an exceedingly popular preacher, and has a very peculiar mind. His style and language are different from every other writer; he often uses words which are not to be found in any dictionary. He is a fine classical scholar, and a good theologue. His communications in "The Evangelist" deserve the serious perusal of Presbyterians and Baptists in general.

There has been for some time in the village of Auburn, quite an interesting revival of religion. It commenced under the labors of the Rev. Mr. Orten, Presbyterian, and has extended itself to the different denominations. Many have been added to the Rev. Mr. Hopkin's church.

The Rev. Mr. Whitaker, pastor of the Universalist congregation in Duane street, the oldest of this denomination in the city, has declared, in a letter to the trustees, that he can advocate the doctrine of universal salvation *no* more. He therefore resigns his office, and begs them to renounce the doctrine immediately.

Probably no man has done more to convince the Universalists of the error of their ways, and the falsity of their hopes, than Professor Stuart has by his able and candid articles upon this subject.

It is but recently that the Rev. Mr. Smith, Pastor of the Universalist Church in Hartford, has renounced his former views, and has since received a license to preach from the Orthodox Congregational Association of Salem. How much more important are such conversions, than the conversions to Van Burenism and Harrisonism.

A Revival in Saratoga Springs

New York Herald, May 15, 1840

SARATOGA SPRINGS, May 5, 1840

JAMES GORDON BENNETT, Esq.

Dear Sir:

This place whose immortality may be dated from the publication of your first Saratoga letter, is sadly in want of your kind admonitions to regulate its affairs. You are received here by many, as the oracle of Fashion, Science, Fun and Trade, and your advice would be received and obeyed with more attention and alacrity, than even the thunders of pulpit orater. In our disputes of Literature and Commerce, the Herald is the umpire, and by a reference to it they are settled.

We have just awakened from a six month's slumber, and expect the sight of new faces, and a renewal of life to this now dull scene. This is certainly a beautiful and pleasant place, but the impressions formed from reading your letters have given me, as it were, new eyes to the comprehension of its beauties. The rides, the rambles in the woods, the calm mild scenery in the vicinity, the tall pines nodding and bowing to the breeze around the serpentine walk; all forming a scene of as quiet beauty as can well be found, and appear to have a charm that either the opening spring, or new impressions have given it—The frolics of the villages have been confined to a few balls, and the tamest and dullest of all village parties. In fact, the only relief to the tedium of experience has been a great revival in the Baptist church. It is a curious feature in the practice of this church, that it seizes the coldest weather to commence its operations, and their zeal appears to increase with the fall of the quicksilver,—at freezing, it is fever heat, and at zero it is boiling. There never was any thing to compare in excitement with this last revival; great has been the falling off from the kingdom of Satan, and he has been seen lying in in [sic] the gutter with a jug by his side, his tail wrapped around its neck to keep it from freezing, bemoaning the losses and defects he has met. First and greatest Elder Knapp. When he spoke of that worthy, he is reported to have laughed heartily and said, "Oh, that Bennett! Oh that picture!" There was one of Knapp's Albany proselytes, a young woman, who, seized with a deep conviction of her unworthiness, and the still greater unworthiness of her neighbors, called on the Deacons of the church and told them they were all sinners, and neglecting God's work, &c. &c. They examined the thermometer, and concluding it to be a favorable time, set to work, hammer and tongs, dealing out damnation and cold water baths with unsparing bounty. The Elder worked night and day, used any quantity of white handkerchiefs, and spoiled the stiffening of divers shirt collars with the reeking perspiration of holiness that poured from his face in a stream which must have been extremely gratifying to the sight and olfactories of the saints. The groaning and sighing, the pushing, jamming, pinching and squeezing, was horrible, the odor of holiness was delightful, especially in the vicinity of the more darkened part of the congregation. The vials of wrath were poured out; the watch dog of the flock backed the sheep into the fold, the stray doves of the Ark were lured into its cover by the promises of salvation; till night after night the "anxious seats" were filled to overflowing. Their "experience" or reasons for their hope, were very interesting—one dreamed that his head was a cabbage head, and that Jesus came in the shape of a spotted cow and bit it off; this opened his eyes to his lust and dreadful state inasmuch as the former part of it was so near the truth, and he became a convert. One "weary rev'rend" Elder who can vie with Knapp in making awful faces, and who has been preaching the Gospel for the last seven years, has just awakened to a deep conviction that he has been a hypocrite and a sinner, and has never known Jesus. The female experiences were very interesting, interlarded with pious ejaculations. "I feel I am a lost sinner." "God is too good to look at an evil creature like me." "I have a hope in a Saviour"—"I aint ashamed to own my Jesus," &c. &c. The sweet angels nearly filled the anxious seats, without aid from he creatures. Sunday after Sunday the cold bathing process was going on much to our amusement, and no doubt the salvation of those who were dipped. God knows they deserved it. The Elder stood up to his middle in the water, singing and crying for more to come to glory; it was curious to witness the efficient manner of their going and coming to the pool; they were passed down like empty buckets and handed out like full ones, when two of the sisters or brothers seized and supported the dipper to a house near by. There seemed, however, a very christian wish that some of them should have a full measure of salvation, one in particular, a sturdy knight of the sledge hammer appeared to need the ablution morally and personally so much, that when he was immersed, there was a general cry from the multitude of "hold him under!" There were at least fifty, some say sixty, brought into the fold of Christs lambs; of course there is some backsliding, but none of note except the false step of one of the most immediate brothers, with a dearly beloved sister; the hero, who is a Santrado in appearances and profession had been administering to the wants of a widowed sister, and is now burthened with a little responsibility. The church are up in arms to defend him and the old sisters were about endeavering to prove that it is impossible for one of the elect to commit a *faux pas*; the young ones only smile and say it originated in *hate of* Christ's children.

There are many things worthy of note I would wish to communicate, but am fearful that I have already trespassed too long.

Dear Bennett, yours ever.   M.

8

Anti-Catholicism in 19th-Century America

Like similar stories published in the *Boston Gazette* in 1834, the "Awful Disclosures by Maria Monk," reproduced in the previous chapter, reflected and fueled Protestant fascination and fears that predated the Revolution.

During the First Great Awakening, the Rev. George Whitefield filled his audiences with tales of the "swarms of monks" the Pope was planning to unleash on an unsuspecting and unrepentant America. His contemporary, the Rev. Jonathan Mayhew, denounced Rome as a filthy prostitute and mother of harlots. In spite of support for the Revolutionary War from Catholic France, Samuel Adams characterized the Church as the "whore of Babylon" in unsigned essays for the *Boston Gazette*. John Adams described it as both Hindu and cabalistic.

As noted in chapter 5, those sentiments fueled the political disputes between the English-supporting federalists and the French-supporting anti-federalists at the turn of the century. With the election of Thomas Jefferson as president, religio-political disputes diminished for a time, but anti-Catholicism lingered and then broke out with renewed fury in the 1840s in the wake of Irish Catholic immigration. Rabidly anti-Catholic white Protestants, calling themselves "Native Americans," banded together against the rising tide of Catholic immigrants.

On his visit to America in 1844, Alexis de Tocqueville gathered the impression of America as a land of religious tolerance. But while he was visiting, riots broke out between the Native Americans and the Roman Catholics living in the working-class Kensington district of Philadelphia.

For almost two weeks, the *Herald* provided extensive coverage of the riots. So heavy was that coverage that on May 10, 1844, Bennett apologized that riot coverage had forced postponement of coverage of many annual church meetings. Most of the riot coverage took the side of the Catholic minority.

"Riots in Philadelphia" and "The Philadelphia Riots" show the depth of feeling on both sides. As journalism, they illustrate the increasing emphasis on active newsgathering, factual reporting and vivid writing. At the same time, the second story shows the easy commingling of opinion and news that characterized journalism in the 1840s. In it, the author first comments on the social implications of the riots before adding updated and new information about them.

Together, the Philadelphia riot stories illustrate how newspapers covered and updated breaking news. They also show the speed with which a story could be published in one city and then picked up and republished in another. Although first published in Philadelphia newspapers, they can be found in the more readily available *New York Herald,* from which they are reprinted. "Riots in Philadelphia" was reprinted in a 3 p.m. extra edition. "The Philadelphia Riots" also arrived in New York in time for the 3 p.m. edition.

In the wake of the riots, Bennett published his own commentaries on the riots and the danger of mixing religion and politics on May 9, 11 and 22. He also published the full text of New York Catholic Bishop John Hughes's pastoral letter on the riots on May 22. However, he continued to criticize the Roman Catholic Church and Bishop Hughes for meddling in congregational affairs, for attempting to make Catholic teachings part of the public school curriculum, and for encouraging Catholics to form their own voting block. Noteworthy examples of that coverage of Catholicism in America can be found in the *Herald* on stories on May 24, May 25, June 4, July 12 and December 23.

On August 7, 1844, Bennett printed an open letter to candidates for president and vice president calling on them to renounce the Native American platform and the use of religion for political purposes. Despite his admonitions, the mixing of religion and politics persisted, causing Bennett to write the bitter commentary, "The Bible in the Election."

Although the Native American, or Know Nothing Party as it came to be called, did not capture the presidency; by the 1850s the Know Nothings controlled most governments in Pennsylvania. As Protestant fears that the growing number of Catholics in America would be loyal to the Pope rather than to America grew, efforts intensified to use public schools to indoctrinate Catholic children in Americanism, that is Protestantism.

In the editorial "Dr. Cheever on the Bible in Schools," Horace Greeley reproduces arguments on both sides of that question that remain relevant today. However, in spite of opposition from leading papers such as the *Tribune* and *Herald,* for decades the Protestant majority remained intent on using the schools to promote Protestantism. One such effort is documented in "Trouble in the Wigwam" reproduced from the church-owned

Deseret News in Salt Lake City; Latter-day Saint leaders had their own reasons for concern.

Riots in Philadelphia

The Kensington Riots—Renewed Hostilities and Awful Destruction of Life and Property—The Native Americans and Irish Catholics

Spirit of the Times, May 8, 1844

Our city is a general scene of alarm and confusion—Kensington is the theatre of an unprecedented riot, of conflagration and bloodshed—the fruits of the quarrel between the Native Americans and the Irish Catholics. We have only room to continue the account of death and devastation commenced yesterday, confining ourselves to the facts as we can gather them, without comment.

During the forenoon of yesterday the scene of Monday's disturbance was remarkably quiet for the time and circumstances, most of the poor Irish were leaving their houses, and moving what they could of their property. At the corners and in the squares around the battle ground were collected crowds of Native Americans, conversing with much excitement upon the doings of Monday, and ready at a moment, to join in a general riot.

About ten o'clock a large party of Native Americans assembled at Second and Master streets, and marched in procession through the district of Kensington, passing the Market House where the fight took place on Monday evening and last night. In the procession was carried the large flag which had been raised on Monday, and which was considerably torn. Preceding this was a banner borne by one man, and having upon its front this inscription:

THIS IS THE FLAG THAT HAS BEEN
TRAMPLED UPON
BY THE IRISH PAPISTS!

The procession moved down Third street to the heart of the city, and cheered at some of the newspaper offices—groaning others.

In the afternoon the Natives assembled in Independence Square, numbering from two to three thousand. A meeting was organized, and the crowd was addressed by Mr. C. J. Jack. From thence they proceeded in procession to Kensington, headed by Mr. Jack, and marched to Second and Master streets, then to the Washington street market, where the fights had occurred on Monday. Here they again organized a meeting, and Mr. Jack again mounted the stage to address them. It was then about 5 o'clock P.M.

Immediately after the organization of the meeting, a scene of extraordinary riot commenced, and which, it is alleged, by the parties was commenced, some say, by the Irish—others say by the Natives. We give the account as accurately as possibly, without any wish to side with either party. Some boys who were in the crowd at the market, commenced throwing stones at the Hibernia hose house opposite on Cadwallader street. Some exhibitions of a general outbreak were apparent, and in a few moments a volley of stones and brickbats were thrown by both parties. There were several small wood houses adjoining the hose house, occupied by Irish people, and at and into the windows these stones and other missiles were thrown. The riot now increased with fearful violence, and one or two guns were fired. It is said that the first shot was from the house at the corner of Master and Cadwallader streets. A rush was made at the Hibernia hose house, and the Hibernia hose carriage, and an old carriage belonging to the Washington hose company, were taken out and carried off—both afterwards broken up.

About this time a volley was fired by the Irish from the corner house named above, and one or two men were shot. The rioting then broke up in extraordinary confusion. During the first of the riot an Irishman rushed out of a house half a square above the scene of destruction, ran down to within some five to ten rods of the mob and fired, killing one man dead. At this time the mob had, it is believed, no arms, and all fled precipitately, leaving a boy with the flag, which was borne off by him and a man who came to his assistance.

The mob then placed the flag up before a house at the N.E. corner of Second and Master, and, after getting a number of muskets, again repaired to the market house, headed by Peter Albright, who had been shot in the hand. They then paraded on the space west and south of the market house, exposed to the shots of the Irish in the houses opposite. A general and bloody skirmish now took place. The natives numbered from thirty to sixty armed men, and they were all who came into the bloody arena. The rest—numbering from five to eight thousand, blocked up every avenue and street leading to the market.

As soon as the armed men appeared in front of the Irish houses, volley after volley was fired into them, and the fire was returned, but with little effect, as the assailed were in a great measure sheltered. This lasted nearly an hour, during which upwards of twenty men of the Natives were shot—probably near half that number killed. Several of the Irish were wounded, but it is not known how many, or whether any of them were killed. Several times, they sallied out in small numbers, and fired upon the Natives, retreating immediately into the houses.

One daring fellow named John Taggart, rushed out of a house, and fired several times upon the Natives—it is said, killed two or three men. A rush was made upon him, and he was captured, though fighting like a madman, and just in the act of shooting a fourth gun. The weapon was wrested from him by a citizen named Bartholomew Baker, and the infuriated mob rushed upon him, knocking him down, and stamping his face almost to shapelessness. Some of the more humane got possession of Taggart, and took him to the ofice of Ald Boileau, in Second street above Beaver—Several times on the way, and even at the office, the infuriated Americans rushed on the Irishman and beat and stamped him most unmercifully. Ald. B. made out a commitment for Taggart, on a charge of murder, and he was given into the hands of citizens to be sent to the Mayor's office of the N. Liberties. They had not proceeded far, however, when another rush was made—those who had charge of him were beaten off, and a most revolting scene followed. The prisoner was kicked and stamped until hardly a feature was discernable; then dragged, by a rope tied round his neck, down the street to the Second street market above Brown. Here the mob attempted to hang him up, but citizens interfered, and after some delay he was borne off to the office of Mayor Cannon, still breathing.

While this was going on, the Natives had been fearfully industrious at the scene of terror. About 6 o'clock, almost every attempt at opposition ceased, and they had it all their own way. The frame house at the corner of Master and Cadwallader streets was broken open and set fire to, and the flames soon spread to the Hose House on Cadwallader street, and several frame houses on Masters street. The armed Natives patroled the streets in front to prevent any attempt to extinguish the flames, and every now and then a gun was fired from the burning buildings and the fire was returned trebly by the crowd.

We left the scene of destruction at at [sic] half-past 7 o'clock P.M. At that time six or eight buildings were in flames and the fire was rapidly spreading. The scene was awfully terrible, and there was a dreadful silence in that vast mob of thousands—broke only by the roar of the flames, the discharges of musketry, and now and then a hoarse hurrah! at some new success of the Natives—that was more alarming than the tumult of battle. The fire balls had been tolling for an hour, and several companies had repaired towards the conflagration, but were all stopped three or four squares off.

We hasten towards the close of this soul-sickening detail—hardly half relating the events of the last ten hours. The following are the names of the killed and wounded, which our reporters have gathered up to this time. They are yet at the scene of carnage, and their return may swell the list.

Charles Rinedollar, ship carpenter, lived in Front st., near Green. Shot in the back of the left shoulder—ball came out of right breast. Died almost instantly.

George Young of Southwark—shot through the left breast—supposed to be mortally wounded.

Augustus Peale, dentist, lives at 176 Locust street, left arm broken by a ball.

Mathew Hammet, ship carpenter, lived in Crown street, Kensington, over 50 years of age, shot through the head, and died instantly. He was fighting desperately at the time.

C. Salisbury, residence not known, shot in the arm.

Charles Stivel, aged about 23, rope maker, lived in Carpenter street above Fifth, Southwark, shot in the neck from above, the ball passing through his lungs and heart—died instantly.

Henry Heiselbaugh, keeper of the Hand-in-hand Tavern, Third and Poplar streets, shot in the fleshy part of the hand.

James Whittaker, lives in Front street, below Spruce, shot in the thigh, the ball striking the bone—bad wound.

Charles Orte, lives in Apple street, near Brown, shot in the head with a slug—very bad wound, not considered dangerous.

John Loeser, lives in Shackamaxon street, Kensington, shot through the left breast—mortally wounded.

Lewis Grebble, lived in Christian street, Southwark, shot in the forehead, brains literally dashed out.

William H. Hillman, turner, lives in Kose Alley, back of School street, Northern Liberties, shot through the body, dangerously wounded

Wright Artiss, ship carpenter, shot through the thigh, badly wounded.

S. Abbott Lawrence, Massachusetts, struck in the breast by a ball; life saved by a penny which was in his vest pocket. The penny was much bent, and he was stunned by the blow. He was merely a spectator.

Willis H. Blaney, ex-Lieut. of Police—shot in the heel—slight wound. P. Albright, of Kensington, shot in the hand—slight wound.

A large man, six feet or more high, was carried off very badly wounded, name not ascertained.

A keeper of a dry goods store in Second street below Pine, shot in the leg, flesh wound; name understood to be Perry or Pierry.

A lad, half grown, shot in the groin, bad wound; name not ascertained.

Another lad shot through the lower part of the abdomen, killed instantly; name unknown.

Another lad, name not known; struck in the breast by a spent ball; flesh wound.

These are all we have heard of up to this time, but there are doubtless more. It is said that three Irishmen were shot and burned in their house; we are not sure of the fact.

The First Division of the Military, under command of Gen. Geo. Cadwallader, and the Sheriff's posse, proceeded to the scene of riot.

NINE O'CLOCK P.M.—We have just left the dreadful yet picturesque scene. The market houses are all in flames and quite a row of brick and frame dwellings whose frighted occupants have fled in all directions for safety and for life. The dark red clouds are lighting up with a horrid glare the blue and quiet sky. Rolls of bright smoke taking fantastic shapes thicken the air, while here and there through the dense crowd the flame tongues of living light may be seen licking with fire some new building preparatory to its destruction. In front may be seen congregations of excited men, shouting, talking, arguing, blustering, and tossing their arms in the air with vehement agitation. Beyond on that open space the plumed heads of glittering swords of the cavalry are waving and glancing in the lurid light, while the heavy tread of men, and the ringing clank of muskets betoken the near presence of the infantry. The adjacent streets are deserted. The houses are closed and abandoned. Since the approach of the military all is still, save that here and there the shriek of a child, or the sob of a woman, or the deep oath of a man break the solemn stillness.

Dim figures move suspiciously in the shade as if seeking concealment, while wretched looking beings driven from their abodes, houseless and homeless, are stealing off with beds, pillows, chairs and tables upon their shoulders, looking for some distant place of deposit. Hark!—a shot!—a scream!—a rush of the soldiers!—and another victim is borne away for surgical assistance. A solitary one horse cart, as we leave, is turning away, and in it are a woman, two girls, a boy, and an infant, all crying. It contains some furniture, and by its side walks a man, who turns back to waste one lingering gaze on the burning pile at hand; and with a groan of intense agony, exclaims, "the toil of twenty years all gone in one moment! My God! have I deserved this!" The cart drove on, and we heard no more. We walked homeward thinking can it be possible that this is a land of Freedom, a land of Laws, a land of Christianity.

TEN O'CLOCK P.M.— We have just learned that an Irish weaver named Joseph Rice, a dweller in one of the houses assaulted in Cadwallader street, but who is said to have taken no part in the contest, was shot through the head while looking over the fence to see how the riot progressed. We looked at the corpse as it lay mangled on the floor of its late habitation, with none save a weeping widow and two fatherless children, sitting in agony beside it. It was a shocking picture.

A man named John S. Fagan, an American, was shot through the shoulder, the ball coming out at his back. A young man, 22 years of age, named John Shreeves, a painter, living in Front above Green street, was shot through the head, and instantly killed. He was an American, and had only been married three months. A man named Deal was shot in the arm. About 7 o'clock P.M.. a young man returning from his work and passing the scene of action, was badly wounded. A great many others were shot, and several killed, whose names we could not ascertain.

The military arrived on the ground about 8 o'clock, P.M. They consisted of the companies of the first brigade, under Gen. Cadwallader. The Sheriff was also on the ground with a small civil posse. As the military approached the market house, they were fired upon from a house on Washington street, but nobody was hurt. Those who fired the gun—some seven or eight Irishmen—principitately fled, and were not captured. The presence of the military had the effect of restoring an almost immediate quiet.

The military occupied all the vacant ground at the scene of destruction. They were stationed along Master, Cadwallader, and Washington streets, and the Germantown road, with cannon planted at every commanding point. A regular guard was set, and patrolling parties kept in constant motion. About 10 o'clock several of the most active of our fire companies arrived on the ground, and protected by the military went into service, and in about an hour succeeeded in arresting the conflagration. They went quietly to work, and did immense execution. They merit all praise.

ELEVEN O'CLOCK—A few guns are being discharged at intervals in Master street. Military in motion, but no rioters discovered. It is said that from 20 to 30 houses altogether have been consumed, located on Cadwallader, Master and Washington streets—some large handsome dwellings, but generally poor buildings. Nohing is left of the Market house but the brick pillars, with which the standing chimneys of the dwellings look like blackened monuments of anarchy. It is thought that many dead bodies of the Irish were consumed in the burning houses.

MIDNIGHT.—All quiet. The military are on the ground. The fires are all extinguished, and the firemen returning home. We have just learned that about nine o'clock, a group of men standing at the corner of Franklin and Second street, was fired upon by a party of Irishmen who came through Perry street, and under cover of the darkness, discharged their guns at them across the lot, wounding a butcher in the Wharton Market, named Taylor, in the eye, and several other persons seriously.

One of the Irish who fired on Monday night at the School House, at the time young Wright was killed, lost his thumb by the bursting of his musket. The thumb and fragments of the gun were picked up yesterday morning. He was tracked by his blood, but could not be found. The man Taggart who was dragged with a rope and hung until apparently dead, was, it seems, simulating death. When taken to the Northern Liberties police office, he quite recovered, and was able to walk with the officers to Moyamensing prison.

Mr. Hillman has just deceased.

The Philadelphia Riots

The Riots in Kensington—The Irish and the Native Americans

Philadelphia Times, May 9, 1844

The late riots in Kensington between the Native Americans and the Irish Roman Catholics—for the feud is now a *religious* one entirely, conceal the fact as we may—have filled out city with excitement, and every thoughtful mind with deep reflection. What are we coming to? Are the people forgetting at once the elements of Republicanism, viz: tolerance of opinion, freedom of thought and action, and obedience to the laws, or can any man engaged in these disgraceful broils believe that he is aiding by such conduct, however provoked, in carrying out the principles of civil and religious liberty?

As a Protestant and a Native born citizen, we protest against this un-natural admixture of religion and politics. In the whole history of the hu-man race, we find the bloodiest pages those in which are recorded the contest of the Church; are we willing to introduce this fire-brand of de-struction and desolation into the midst of our peaceful and happy coun-try? Have we a mind to rival Europe in our chronicles of inhuman mas-sacre and slaughter, or shall we bathe our hearth-stones in blood, and make our homes charnel-houses, because of differences of opinion, the entertainment of which is guaranteed to every American citizen, whether Native-born or Naturalized, by our glorious Constitution?

We are opposed to the political sentiments of the Native Americans, but we respect their sincerity, and would be the last to stand silently by and see them insulted; to see their peaceable assemblies broken up by an unfuriated multitude, and see them or any other set of men, whether right or wrong in their views, waylaid and assaulted for promulgating their political notions. We are too much of a Republican, and have too much genuine American feeling for this; but, we are equally opposed to the introduction of religious abuse into political orations; we entertain a very contemptuous opinion of the wisdom, the law-and-order-loving dis-positions, and the *real* Christianity of those demagogues who do it to ac-complish, by the fearful public orgasm which must follow, their own selfish ends.

We give up to n[o] man in our respect for the Bible, and our zeal for its dissemination. We up to no man in our love for our beloved country, its unparalleled institutions, its mighty and intelligent people, and above all its freedom for that curse of Europe, an union of Church and State. But, in tenaciously reserving for ourselves and our children the right to peruse the Bible, we should be the first to rebel against any attempt to coerce others into its perusal; in jealously watching to prevent the politi-cal dominance of any other religious persuasion, we should be among the first to denounce any attempt at such dominance contemplated by the members of our own.

These are the dictates of patriotism; nay more, they are the dictates of

Christianity. Without pretending to take any side in this unfortunate controversy—without pretending that the Roman Catholics are right or wrong, or that the Native Americans are right or wrong, for we concive [sic] both to have committed a grievous error in appealing under any circumstances to physical force or to arms,—let us ask, is such conduct characteristic of either Freemen or Christians? Is it the part of a true republican to thrust his opinions upon others, and to picture all those who differ from him as fit subjects for immolation; or did the great prototype of the Christian church when on earth set his followers such a belligerant example? Was not the language of the latter always "peace? peace?" Was not his course exemplarily pacific? Did he turn even on his revilers and persecutors? Did he not take every occasion to teach his disciples forbearance, and radically subdue in them the slightest impulse towards retaliation?

If so, we are bound to follow the example as well as the advice of the head of the Universal Christian Church! And in doing so, we at once carry out the principles of good government, for republicanism and christianity are identical, and the very spirit of the one, is incorporated into and animates the other. Let us have *peace* then. Cease these wicked contentions. And in order that they may cease, stop at once this mingling together of religion and politics. Away with it. It is an unhallowed, an iniquitous, and an incestuous union. The issue must be a monster, misshapen and deplorable, inimical to liberty, repulsive to tranquil government, and ever associated with but anarchy, discord, murder, and civil war.

The mob then insisted that he should dismiss every Irishman from the city police. He said he had made no appointments except of naturalized citizens, &c, according to law. If there was any fault it was in the law. The First City Troop under Capt. Butler then came up, and after parading around, retired towards Kensington. Quiet ensued for a moment—then the mob rushed at the police, drove them back—pelted the church windows with stones—then lifted two boys over the iron railing who climbed into the buildings by a window that had been broken, and while one set fire to the curtains with a match another cut the gas pipe thus putting the church into a blaze in a few moments!

The police then rallied, and made several arrests. The two boys were captured, but immediately rescued by the Natives. So were the rest. The police were severely beaten in the attempt to retain the prisoners. One of the night police, named Long, was much injured by a brick bat. A pistol was wrested from the hands of another officer. An immense crowd soon gathered. The firemen arrived and played on the adjoining houses, some of which were partially burned. The church burned slowly, lighting up the whole city with its blaze, while thousands from all quarters stood gazing on calmly at the work of destruction.

11 O'CLOCK, P.M.—St. Augustine's Church is entirely consumed, and the multitude dispersed. St. Mary's, St. Joseph's, and St. John's churches have been filled with armed men, and as their demolition is threatened, people are gathering around them and in them waiting for the assault. The two first churches are guarded outside by three companies of the 2d brigade, under Col. Goodman. The troops occupy Fourth street, from Walman to Spruce. A party of the Philadelphia Greys have just brought to the Mayor's office, arrested at Kensington, a boy named Hess, taking in the act of communicating fire to a house.

The City Councils have just met.

Order it is said, have been sent down to Fort Mifflin for U.S. soldiers. The City is all in confusion. Nothing but vigourous efforts which cannot be expected from the Volunteers, or the Civil posse will prevent Philadelphia from becoming a prey to the mob, and preventing a general conflagration!

12 o'clock.—The Governor is said to have just arrived in town, and to have declared the City of Philadelphia under MARTIAL LAW!

THURSDAY MORNING, 1 o'clock.—The Catholic Churches throughout the City are now protected by Companies of Volunteers. The whole of the First Division has arrived from Kensington leaving that District to the care of two Companies of Germantown Volunteers. The citizens of Kensington are in great alarm in consequence, and are sending down to the city for aid. Gen. Cadwallader and the First Brigade are at St. John's Church. Military patrols walk the streets, and every thing wear the aspect of war. The City Councils are still in secret session with the Sheriff.

TWO O'CLOCK A.M.—The Mayor, in the melee at St. Augustine church last night, was struck in the abdomen with a brick bat, and rendered insensible for an instant. The only person who stuck to him was a thief.

The mob were dispersed from St. John's church by the military— Gen. Cadwallader giving them but five minutes to leave the ground, at the peril of being fired upon. The artillery are now guarding St. John's church, the State arsenal opposite, and the Orphan Asylum, Chestnut street, Market, Thirteenth and Chesnut streets are full of the artillerists and their field-pieces.

The infantry are at the other churches. Private Hartnett, of the State artillery, was accidentally shot through the leg while marching up to Kensington in the afternoon.

The Bible in the Election

The New York Herald, December 27, 1844

The party at present in the ascendency in the corporation are preparing to sustain themselves in the election next spring. Their policy is very curious and very amusing. During the last few months that they have been in office, they have abandoned with the utmost coolness and impudence every single principle of reform to which they solemnly pledged themselves before the election. They have increased the city taxation enormously—they have refused us police reform—they have kept the streets in an alarmingly filthy condition—they have continued all the old corrupt system of job work—in a word, they have proved themselves to be the most worthless, inefficient and imbecile rulers whose burden the city has ever been called to endure.

But the dominant party in the corporation have, it appears, a weapon to employ, by the help of which they are confident of retaining power, and being enabled to impose upon the community for another year. They are going to make a great noise about "the Bible"—they are going to bring that holy volune into the polluted arena of the dirty politics of this city. If any one complains of increased taxation, they will call out in reply—"the Bible! the Bible!" If we talk about the dirty streets, they will silence us with—"the Bible! the Bible!" If we ask for a good police, they will shout out—"the Bible! the Bible!"—All this will not avail men who have been false to every promise. The Bible teaches men to abide by the truth, and to fulfil their engagements; and it also warns us to beware of those who have once deceived us. The people will soon discover that they are quite prepared to discover a practical adherence to this maxim of the Bible, at least.

Dr. Cheever on the Bible in Schools

New-York Daily Tribune, February 28, 1854

The Education of the Whole People, everywhere most important, is, in a Democracy an imperative necessity. To be led by the blind among treacherous pitfalls, over dizzy hights [sic] and beside unfathomable chasms, involves perils only less formidable than those of unlimited Despotism. Whatever elements of weakness or mischief may be discovered in our political system flow directly from the incompetency of a portion of our people for the momentous duties thereby devolved on them; and we cannot remember an instance where our Government has been popularly impelled into a wrong course wherein it was not manifest that the mischief had been done by a large majority of our uneducated voters overruling a majority of those who had enjoyed the advantages of at least rudimental instruction. If the education of every child were inexorably required and enforced, and each adult migrating to our shores were subjected to a similar requisition as a qualification for voting, in lieu of the present exaction of five years' residence, the basis of our political fabric would be as nearly perfect as Humanity in its present estate will permit.

Now the Education of the Whole People otherwise than by a comprehensive, State-supported system of Common Schools, has been abundantly proved impracticable. They who assert that the Education of Children devolves on the Church, or should be left to the care of the parents respectively, cannot controvert the general fact that, just so far as Education has been cared for by the State, has it been general and efficient, while wherever the State has left it to individuals, voluntarily associated, or to clerical impulse and guidance, a very large proportion of the children of the poor and powerless have been suffered to grow up in ignorance. If there be an exception to this rule, we are not aware of it.

The Patriot, the Liberal, the Philanthropist, the Conservative, the Devotee, would seem to be equally inerested in demanding that the State shall make careful and ample provision for at least the elementary Education of All. For though the Devotee, of whatever creed, cannot hope to have the tenets of his faith expounded and commended to the children attending Common Schools under a Government which is wisely interdicted from the establishment of a State Religion, he should nevertheless be satisfied in view of the fact that the Common School plows up the ground and prepares it for the seed which it is his or his Church's duty to sow. The modern Sunday School, as at first established, was devised by a Christian philanthropist for the purpose of teaching the children of the poor to read, so that they might afterward be indoctrinated in the great truths of religion. The Common School has since superseded this use of the Sunday School, so that the latter is now devoted exclusively to the direct inculcation of religious and moral lessons. And this seems to us the natural and proper solution of the great problem of Universal Education in communities where radical diversities of faith exist. Let the Common School, for thirty hours of each week, instruct the children in Reading, Writing, Grammar, Geography, Arithmetic, &c. and let these children, thus qualified to receive and apprehend religious truth, be instructed in religion on Saturday, Sunday, or during any other than school hours on other days, by such clerical or other teachers as their respective parents or guardians may prefer and indicate.

But shall there be no religious exercises in Common Schools? Our choice would be that a brief prayer should be offered and a select portion of Scripture read by the teacher and a hymn of praise to the Father of All sung by the entire school; perhaps the two former at the beginning, the latter at the close of the day's lessons. But we recognize the Rights of Conscience as above all considerations of choice or convenience, and we should most strenuously protest against these or any other religious exercises in any school where they would grate on the religious convictions, sensibilities, or if you please, prejudices of any portion of the pupils or their natural guardians. Rather let every exercise of a religious nature be remitted to other occasions than have one parent feel that the faith he cherishes is endangered or undermined by the inculcations or disciplines of the Common School. Whenever this shall become the school of a predominant Church, or of a local Majority, then will its usefulness be fatally undermined and its hold on the confidence of the people be seriously weakened.

The Reverend Doctor George B. Cheever holds a theory very different from this. In his view, those who desire to have certain religious exercises in Schools have as good a right to insist on their introduction as those who object to such exercises, and whose faith would be assailed thereby, have to require their exclusion. In other words, if there were a sect who made pork-eating a part of their religious exercises, and they were a majority, it would be perfectly right for that majority to force their pork-eating into a common school where a minority of the children were Hebrews, and insist that those children should swallow the pork or be kicked out of school. Nay: if we do not misapprehend the Doctor, he believes the pork-eating majority, if they were orthodox in their faith, would have a *better* right to make pork-eating a common school exercise than the minority would to resist it. Hear him:

"The case stands thus: You either know this book to be the Word of God, or you do not; if not, then you are engaged in a solemn farce in teaching it any where as God's Word. But if you do know it to be God's Word, then you have no right to put a book of fables on an equality with it;—you have no right to permit the plea of another man's conscience as against it, to prevent you from violating it, wherever you have the proper opportunity and the power. If you know this book to be the Word of God, you cannot, without a glaring inconsistency, which is fatal to the claims of God's Word, admit the conscience of a Mohammedan or Pagan as of equal authority with the conscience of a man instructed out of God's Word. The conscience which commands the worship of idols is not to be treated with the same respect as the conscience which commands the worship of God. If you say that it is, you are instantly driven to the most dreadful conclusions, fatal to the very existence of Christian society."

Surely, no one can fail to see that here is the assumption of an Established Religion already existing in the land, whose adherents have rights under our laws superior to those of all dissenters. And Mr. Cheever proceeds to quote Judge Story as authority for the assertion that it is the duty of our Government to foster and encourage the diffusion of Christianity among all our citizens, and to aid in setting forth "the great doctrines of religion," among which he enumerates a *future* "state of rewards and punishments." We take this as an illustration of the dangerous and utterly un-American tendency of Mr. Cheever's project. We believe that men will suffer in a future state of being on account of the evil they have done in this life; but some of the purest men and best Christians we have ever known understand the Bible to teach that all sin is limited to this life, and that all sin here committed is here inexorably punished. By what right—on what principle consistent with our Constitutional guarantee that "Congress shall make no law respecting the establishment of religion, or prohibiting the free exercise thereof," with the corresponding provisions in all or most of our State Constitutions—shall money be taxed out of these citizens for the support of schools wherein their children are to be taught theological dogmas which they earnestly regard as borrowed from ancient Paganism and at war with the fundamental basis of Christianity? If a small minority may be thus treated, who can feel secure in the immunity hitherto enjoyed by *his* religious convictions? If to-day the Common School may teach that the punishment of sin committed here is wholly or partly postponed to another life, may they not to-morrow be engaged in the inculcation of Roman Catholic or Lutheran, Trinitarian or Socinian, Baptist or Methodist tenets, as the majority may see fit to prescribe? And how much longer will they deserve the name of *Common* Schools?

True, Mr. Cheever seems to be animated by a special hostility to the Catholics, against whom his batteries are generally pointed, while he is professedly pleading only for the unqualified use of the Bible in Schools; but one must be blind indeed who does not see that the scope of his argument is far broader, and tends virtually to the recognition of a legally established Religion, to be based, as nearly as practicable, on his own ideas of what the State Religion should be. To such an establishment we are sure a large majority of the American people are sternly opposed, and not even the cry of "No Popery!" potent as that is, will suffice to swerve them from their settled convictions.

No one can need to be told that our religious views differ widely, radically, from those of the Roman Catholics, with whose Hierarchy the march of events in Europe has involved us in a conflict which the future is likely to aggravate. Roman Catholics as a class do not take THE TRIBUNE, and we presume they never will; they do not vote with us, and that we suppose will generally if not always remain so. We mean to deserve their respect, with that of all other citizens, by speaking the truth fearlessly and standing firm for Equal Rights to All: but their favor and patronage is neither sought nor expected by us. Yet it is but simple justice to say that Mr. Cheever's incessant representations that Roman Catholics dread the Bible, fear the Bible, or as he says on page 36, *"hate the Bible,"* are in our view false and calumnious. The only Catholic family wherein we ever lived had an open Bible in its parlor throughout our stay in it; and this was more than twenty years ago, before any collision with regard to the Bible in schools had been developed in this City. In almost every Catholic journal we glance over, we see editions of the Bible advertised for sale, and commended to Catholics by their Archbishops and Bishops; and these facts are to our mind utterly inconsistent with the assumption that they either hate the Bible or dread its dissemination.

That they may object to the use of the Bible as a school reader, especially if a version be used which their Church has condemned as erroneous and heretical, by no means justifies Mr. Cheever's imputations,
which seem only calculated to fan the fires of sectarian bigotry and increase the bitterness of religious hatreds.

It is in this view that we ask the attention of all earnest, intelligent
friends of Universal Education to the doctrines and spirit of Mr.
Cheever's book. Surely, no discerning person can fail to see that this
spirit, if allowed to dominate, will prove fatal to all hopes of the mainte-
nance of Common Schools. We hear it asserted that the Catholic priesthood are hostile to our Common Schools, and mean to withdraw the
Catholic children therefrom as fast as possible. If such be the fact, Mr.
Cheever is helping them efficiently, and only needs to become suffi-
ciently influential with Protestants to insure the meditated consummation. For whenever the spirit which animates his book shall predominate
in the management of our Common Schools, Catholic parents will be
driven, by self-respect if nothing else, to take their children away, and
give them such education as they can find elsewhere. Ignorance is a
calamity, and to pay twice for an education a hardship, but better even
this than to submit tamely to insult, misrepresentation, and a wanton attack on profoundly cherished convictions respecting the most momentous theme that can fix the attention of Man.

Trouble in the Wigwam

Deseret News, March 18, 1855

[Correspondence of the *Evening Post*]

BOSTON, January 12, 1855

Our Legislature is hard at work to convince its constituents that Popery and foreigners are to receive no quarter at its hands. Already several
orders have been introduced bearing against the Catholics.

There was an order adopted on Wednesday, instructing the Judiciary
Committee to consider the expediency of reporting a bill making con-
vents, or nunneries, and Roman Catholic schools as open and free to
public visitation and inspection as Protestant institutions.

The Committee on Education, the same day, was instructed to inquire into the expediency of altering laws, so as to provide that every child between the ages of eight and fourteen, whether of native or foreign birth, be compelled to attend the public schools at least twelve weeks in the year.

This last proposition, however, will hardly come to anything, as it is calculated to play the very deuce with the truest and bluest Protestants in the state. The passage and enforcement of a law containing such a provision would break up all the private establishments for education in Massachusetts, so far as they are attended by children between the ages of eight and twelve years.

The interference which this order contemplates on the part of the state, in the private affairs of families, may be suited to the latitude of Prussia; but it will not answer for this bleak part of the world.

The reformers will find much difficulty in hitting Catholics hard without cutting down five times the number of Protestants.

Perhaps it is as well that it should be so, in order to prevent us from becoming rampant.

A third order contemplates the daily reading of the common English version of the Bible in all of the public schools of the state, or at least of restricting the school fund appropriation of the state to such schools, and only such, as shall comply with such daily practice. This is bringing up of an old question, and one out of which the whigs made a great deal of capital in 1853, when the new constitution was voted down, principally because the Irish Catholics did not like a provision providing against the public support of sectarian schools, and which was not in the body of the instrument. It is a queer sight to see that of a gentleman who called upon the Catholics to vote against the provision named, now demanding that such people shall be excluded from voting, and be compelled to send their children to Protestant schools. Their opinion and their practice have been wonderfully changed. Perhaps they are resolved to keep his Excellency strictly in countenance.

Yesterday the Judiciary Committee were ordered to consider the expediency of reporting an amendment to the constitution, providing that any man owing allegiance to any foreign power, either civil or ecclesiastical, shall not be eligible to any office in Massachusetts. The object is to place the Catholics on the same footing that they now occupy in New Hampshire.

The signal given by the Governor for war upon the Catholics has been heartily responded to. We seem to be on the eve of civil and religious troubles like those of which we have read in history, without deeming it possible that such things would ever threaten the peace of an American state.

The reports of Mr. J. R. Lowell's lecture in the 'Daily Advertiser' are made from the author's manuscript, by a distinguished literary gentleman of Cambridge, and can therefore be depended upon for correctness and finish. The first lecture was admirable, and the whole course will probably be of the same character.

9

The Mormon Question

The Second Great Awakening unleashed a wave of religious fervor that once again divided families and split churches and paved the way for new ones. Some of those new churches were well within the Christian tradition; other religious movements were not. For mainstream Protestants, however, the most troubling and perplexing of the upstart religions was that of the Church of Jesus Christ of Latter-day Saints.

The Church traces its origins to 1821 when its founder, Joseph Smith, first claimed to have had visions that included a visit from a messenger of God, Moroni, who revealed to him a hidden book of golden plates and special stones through which Smith could read and translate the writings. Those writings, the *Book of Mormon,* told of America as a special place. They also gave to those who accepted the new revelation an important role in furthering God's plan for the world.

Smith's message that those who believed were saints and would rule struck a responsive chord, particularly among the poor and disadvantaged. Others, however, saw the Mormon religion as a dangerous heresy with the potential to undermine traditional Christianity. As the new religion attracted converts, fears of it grew. The Mormons were driven from New York to Ohio, Missouri, and then to Nauvoo, Illinois.

In Illinois, the tightly knit Mormon communities prospered, but they invited envy and raised fears that the Mormons, voting as a block, would influence elections and establish a theocracy. When Joseph Smith announced in 1843 that he had received a new revelation sanctioning plural marriage and then in 1844 that he would seek the presidency, those fears escalated. On the night of June 27, 1844, a mob marched on the Nauvoo jail. There, someone shot Smith, who was being held on charges related to destruction of a printing press that had been used to publish anti-Mormon sentiments.

Before his death, Smith and his followers had received scattered and mixed attention in the *New York Herald* and other major newspapers. The murder was a major story, but it, too, produced mixed coverage. In "The Mormon Massacre," James Gordon Bennett takes the side of the threatened religious minority, just as he took the side of the Irish Catholics in the Philadelphia riots. In "The Mormon Massacre," he once again describes the combining of religion and politics, mixed with jealousy and prejudice as the root causes of the massacre. Although Bennett used the occasion to again attack other newspapers for their role in inflaming public opinion, he also opened his paper to other viewpoints. News from "Carthage" begins by mimicking Bennet's style. However, in contrast to Bennet's opinion about the massacre, the correspondent from Illinois attacks the eastern press as he justifies the massacre.

Shortly before his death, Joseph Smith had written that the Mormons should "secure a resting place in the mountains, or some uninhabited region, where we can enjoy the liberty of conscience guaranteed to us by the Constitution of our country." In 1846, under their new leader, Brigham Young, the Latter-day Saints set off for Utah, where their community once again flourished.

On his trip west in 1859, Horace Greeley, one of the most influential newspaper editors of his time, provided readers of his *New-York Daily Tribune* with on-the-scene reports from the Mormon territory. The first of those, "Two Hours with Brigham Young," is one of the first, if not the first, examples of the question-answer format for reporting on an interview. In it, Greeley tries to give a faithful, accurate account of Mormon theology. At the same time, the questions reveal as much about Greeley's interests and concerns as those of the Mormons.

The critical commentary Greeley appended to the transcript of the interview captures the prevalent view that the Mormon practice of plural marriage threatened morality and the social order. That view persisted even after renunciation of the practice paved the way for Utah statehood. In January 1900, Congress refused to seat Brigham H. Roberts as Utah's duly elected representative because he had refused to abandon his wives. Accounts of the debate in the House of Representatives can be found in many papers, including the *Topeka Daily Capital,* which published many speeches and Roberts's final statement on January 26.

"Polygamy, Politics, and the Union Pacific Railroad," the final article in this chapter, provides another glimpse of attempts to tame Mormon influence and Mormon counterefforts to protect and preserve their culture. The piece once again points to the kind of Mormon business acumen that so often inspired envy and fueled anti-Mormon prejudices.

The Mormon Massacre

New York Herald, July 12, 1844

Accounts confirmatory of the fact that Joe Smith and his brother were actually massacred—murdered in cold blood, continue to reach us from the West. There can be no doubt that political feeling entered largely into the popular excitement in that region against the Mormons. It was feared by the Whigs that the Nauvoo people would give material aid to Polk. This affords another and most melancholy illustration of the pernicious, demoralizing, brutalizing influence of the party presses, which are daily influencing the passsions of the people by the vilest and most incendiary tirades against their respective opponents.

Besides, Nauvoo was very favorably situated, and from its natural advantages combined with those created by the Prophet, under his singular government, was very rapidly increasing in population and trade, which excited the jealous and envy of the people of Warsaw, a business place a little below Nauvoo. The people of Carthage, also, another trading village or town in the interior, were stimulated by the same feelings to oppose the Mormons. These feelings of enmity arising from accursed envy and avarice, were constantly inflamed by a blackguard paper in Warsaw called the "Signal."

The conduct of the people of Illinois and Missouri towards the Mormons has been brutal and detestable in the extreme, and discovering the same spirit that burned the witches at Salem and the Convent at Boston.

Carthage

The Mormons and their Leader—His Crimes,
Character, and Massacre—Pleas in Palliation—
Anti-Mormon Defence.

New York Herald, September 2, 1844

CARTHAGE, August 11th, 1844

DEAR SIR:

Since I had the pleasure of seeing you, last winter, in your sanctum sanctorum, from whence editorial genius spreads its brightening rays and illuminates the civilized world, I have been playing the cosmopolite, but at last returned to the country of Joe Smith notoriety in time to witness the scenes— the glorious and inglorious achievements of the Mormon war in Hancock county—and as many uninformed correspondents have written for the eastern papers, whose statements are erroneous, in many particulars, in relation to the causes of the death of the Smith's at Carthage, while also many editors are severely rebuking the old citizens of Hancock county, a portion of whom are supposed to be among the perpetrators of the offence, leaving the impression upon the public mind that they are a vindictive set of cut throats, and guilty of one of the foulest murders recorded in the annals of crime, I will relate to you a few facts, being a few of the prominent causes which induced the old citizens of the surrounding country to arise in their indignation and strike the blow which cut off the head of an evil, which to them, and to every freeman within the sphere of its baneful influence, had become intolerable.

First, sir, let me promise that I shall not attempt to justify the course of the perpetrators, but to palliate their conduct by showing the circumstances by which they were surrounded. I know, sir, that the spirit of mobocracy which results in the infliction of summary vengeance or justice is dangerous in its tendency; that it generally rushes beyond the convictions of the community; that it disarms men of reason; that it unbridles and gives free exercise to the baser portions of our nature; but I have been unwillingly convinced of one lamentable fact—that, on the border settlements of our free republic, beyond the influence of a high degree of virtue and refinement, such as exist in older settlements in a new country, where so many bankrupts, in honor and character, are found, who are willing to foster and cherish crime, a case has arose where the slow, uncertain and obstructed operation of the law was not adequate to redress the grievances of an injured and an oppressed community—where the old and honored citizens of the country must either yield as slaves and bow submissive to the will of a despotic, pretended Prophet of the Lord, or grasp the sword of retributive justice, and execute the decree which emanates from the heart of every patriot.

You, doubtless, are acquainted with the past history of the Mormons—how the imposter Joe Smith commenced his pretended divine mission in the State of New York, where he was known as a lazy, idle, thick-headed boy; that he gathered around him a few loafers there, and soon became so obnoxious to the inhabitants there, that they employed means to rid the State of his presence; that from there he went to Kirt-

land, Ohio, and in a few years gathered a considerable number of proselytes; that he there commenced his swindling operations on quite an extensive scale, at a time when the banking system was popular; he successfully demonstrated the proposition that paper currency was unsafe,
after committing outrages there which the good citizens of Ohio were
not disposed to submit to. They gave him a few strikes, which induced
him to pack up and lead his motley crew to the Western borders of the
State of Missouri; there he carried on such a series of agitations which
brought on a bloody war, and resulted in the total extermination of the
Mormons. From there they fled to the hospitable shores of Illinois. Upon
their arrival here, they sung the plaintive song of persecution and oppression for their religious opinions, and being in a state of abject poverty,
the citizens of Illinois contributed liberally for their relief, and established for them a home in their midst. The legislature granted them a
charter for their city, expecting from them professions that they would be
a valuable acquisition to our young populace, little thinking that they
were cherishing a viper that would sting them the moment he was
warmed into life and power.

Let us enquire what has been the situation of the old citizens; the kind
entertainment of a band of strangers; and what the conduct of Joe Smith
and his followers, the recipients of not only kindness and hospitality, but
even honors, from the hands of their new neighbors. They, the Mormons,
instead of adopting principles of action comporting with their professions of Christianity, have outraged every principle of the Christian religion. Joe Smith, assuming the character of a religious reformer, was
practically, a public blasphemer, who often shocked the moral sense of
the christian with his heaven daring declarations of his intimacy with
Deity. Charges were preferred against him and many of his followers, of
being guilty of almost every crime known to our laws, both moral and
municipal, and those charges are susceptible of the most indubiable
proof. Credible witnesses can be had who lived in Nauvoo, some who
were in the confidence of Smith, to whom he would make admissions
and solicit their aid in the destruction of female virtue, and in swindling
his deluded victims out of their property, under pretence that it was the
Lord's will they should yield to the wants and desires of God's Holy
Prophet, or jeapordize their eternal salvation. Other persons in the city
who are unconnected with the Mormon church, have been close observers of Smith's conduct during the existence of the city of Nauvoo,
who are acquainted with a chain of circumstances which fixes guilt of

the deepest dye upon him as unerringly as though the knowledge had been derived through the medium of the senses. Still the apologists of the Mormons appear to think the charges against the Mormons are amply disproved by the senseless declarations of a few itinerant news-gatherers, who seem to think they are the cause of the world preserving its proper equilibrium, by their attending to the business of others and reporting upon the state of the public mind in the different quarters of the globe—they come to Nauvoo, anxious to ascertain for themselves the facts in relation to the Mormons; they of course would go to the source of Mormon truth, Joe Smith. He immediately sees they are strangers, and shrewdly suspects their business; he treats them politely, takes them in his carriage, shows them the curiosities of the city, the exhibitions of industry among the citizens; speaks of his persecutors; says the true church always was persecuted; appeals to God that he is innocent of crime and free from all unrighteousness. The stranger, if he does not go down to the water and be baptized, he goes away satisfied that the poor Mormons are an injured people, and those who are opposed to them are maddened by the demon of prejudice. Of course, those astute philosophers, to become satisfied of the truth of the charges made against Smith and his adherents, would expect them to confess their crimes to them and practice their iniquities at noon-day, in the presence of strangers. I hope some of the institutions of the East will note those gentlemen benefactors of the age, and reward them with a leather medal apiece.

The citizens in the immediate neighborhood of the Mormons are not destitute of intelligence. It is to them the people must look for correct information in relation to their own difficulties; either they or the Mormons must tell the tale. It is a question of veracity between them—that question can be settled by viewing the circumstances. The old citizens of Hancock have always heretofore enjoyed an enviable reputation. How does the case stand with the Mormons? Let their past history answer! Can it be possible that a large portion of the people of New York, Ohio, Missouri and Illinois, are unworthy the appelation of American citizens, and that Joe Smith was a true prophet, and a paragon of excellence? The historian of our country may answer the question.

The question will be asked, why was not the Smiths punished by law? I am obliged to answer briefly, as my sheet is nearly full. Joe Smith had the power and the will to defeat entirely the ends of justice in Hancock. He could have a Mormon jury—he could have Mormon witnesses, who were bound by the severest penalties to deliver him from danger, if required the commission of perjury, or murder—he could then with impunity, as he did do, imprison men to gratify his malice,—attack and beat men in the street, for daring to do their duty—virtutally disenfranchise the old citizens of the country, and abuse and vilify them if they dared to say a word against him. He slandered and libelled the character of those in Nauvoo, who established a press to defend themselves, which press was destroyed by Smith's order; he refused to be brought to justice for the offense, for which reason the militia of the State had to be called out at an expense of some $20,000; the people after draining the cup of endurance to the very dregs, arose in their indignation and struck home to the traitor's heart.

THE SPIRIT OF THE NAUVOO EXPOSITER

Two Hours with Brigham Young

New-York Daily Tribune, August 20, 1859

SALT LAKE CITY, Utah, July 13, 1859

Mr friend Dr. Bernhisel, M.C., took me this afternoon, by appointment to meet Brigham Young, President of the Mormon Church, who had expressed a willingness to receive me at 2 P.M. We were very cordially welcomed at the door by the President, who led us into the second story parlor of the largest of his houses (he has three), where I was introduced to Heber C. Kimball, Gen. Wells, Gen. Ferguson, Albert Carrington, Elias Smith, and several other leading men in the Church, with two full-grown sons of the President. After some unimportant conversation on general topics, I stated that I had come in quest of fuller knowledge respecting the doctrines and polity of the Mormon Church, and would like to ask some questions bearing directly on these, if there were no objection. President Young avowed his willingness to respond to all pertinent inquiries, the conversation proceeded substantially as follows:

H.G.—Am I to regard Mormonism (so-called) as a new religion, or as simply a new development of Christianity?

B.Y.—We hold that there can be no true Christian Church without a priesthood directly overmissioned by and in immediate communication with the Son of God and Savior of mankind. Such a church is that of the Latter-Day Saints, called by their enemies Mormons: we know no other that even pretends to have present and direct revelations of God's will.

H.G.—Then I am to understand that you regard all other churches professing to be Christian as the Church of Rome regards all churches not in communion with itself—as schismatic, heretical, and out of the way of salvation?

B.Y.—Yes, substantially.

H.G.—Apart from this, in what respect do your doctrines differ essentially from those of our Orthodox Protestant Churches—the Baptist or Methodist, for example?

B.Y.—We hold the doctrines of Christianity, as revealed in the Old and New Testaments—also in the Book of Mormon, which teaches the same cardinal truths, and those only.

H.G.—Do you believe in the doctrine of the Trinity?

B.Y.—We do; but not exactly as it is held by other churches. We believe in the Father, the Son, and the Holy Ghost, as equal, but not identical—not as one person [being]. We believe in all the Bible teaches on this subject.

H.G.—Do you believe in a personal devil—a distinct, conscious, spiritual being, whose nature and acts are essentially malignant and evil?

B.Y.—We do.

H.G.—Do you hold the doctrine of Eternal Punishment?

B.Y.—We do; though perhaps not exactly as other churches do. We believe it as the Bible teaches it.

H.G.—I understand that you regard Baptism by Immersion as essential.

B.Y.—We do.

H.G.—Do you practice Infant Baptism?

B.Y.—No.

H.G.—Do you make removal to these valleys obligatory on your converts?

B.Y.—They would consider themselves greatly aggrieved if they were not invited hither. We hold to such a gathering together of God's People as the Bible foretells, and that this is the place, and now is the time appointed for its consummation.

H.G.—The predictions to which you refer have usually, I think, been understood to indicate Jerusalem (or Judea) as the place of such gathering.

B.Y.—Yes, for the Jews—not for others.

H.G.—What is the position of your Church with respect to slavery?

B.Y.—We consider it of Divine institution, and not to be abolished until the curse pronounced on Ham shall have been removed from his descendants.

H.G.—Are any slaves now held in this Territory?

B.Y.—There are.

H.G.—Do your Territorial laws uphold Slavery?

B.Y.—These laws are printed—you can read for yourself. If slaves are brought here by those who owned them in the States, we do not favor their escape from the service of their owners.

H.G.—Am I to infer that Utah, if admitted as a member of the Federal Union, will be a Slave State?

B.Y.—No; she will be a Free State. Slavery here would prove useless and unprofitable. I regard it generally as a curse to the masters. I myself hire many laborers and pay them fair wages; I could not afford to own them. I can do better than subject myself to an obligation to feed and clothe their families, to provide and care for them in sickness and health. Utah is not adapted to Slave Labor.

H.G.—Let me now be enlightened with regard more especially to your Church polity: I understand that you require each member to pay over one-tenth of all he produces or earns to the Church.

B.Y.—That is a requirement of our faith. There is no compulsion as to the payment. Each member acts in the premises according to his pleasure, under the dictates of his own conscience.

H.G.—What is done with the proceeds of this tithing?

B.Y.—Part of it is devoted to building temples and other places of worship; part to helping the poor and needy converts on their way to this country; and the largest portion to the support of the poor among the Saints.

H.G.—Is none of it paid to Bishops and other dignitaries of the Church?

B.Y.—Not one penny. No Bishop, no Elder, no Deacon, or other church officer, receives any compensation for his official services. A Bishop is often required to put his hand in his own pocket and provide therefrom for the poor of his charge; but he never receives anything for his services.

H.G.—How, then, do your ministers live?

B.Y.—By the labor of their own hands, like the first Apostles. Every Bishop, every Elder, may be daily seen at work in the field or the shop, like his neighbors; every minister of the Church has his proper calling by which he earns the bread of his family; he who cannot or will not do the Church's work for nothing is not wanted in her service; even our lawyers (pointing to Gen. Ferguson and another present, who are the regular lawyers of the Church), are paid nothing for their services; I am the only person in the Church who has not a regular calling apart from the Church's service, and I never received one farthing from her treasury; if I obtain anything from the tithing-house, I am charged with and pay for it, just as any one else would; the clerks in the tithing-store are paid like other clerks, but no one is ever paid for any service pertaining to the ministry. We think a man who cannot make his living aside from the Ministry of Christ unsuited to that office. I am called rich, and consideer myself worth $250,000; but no dollar of it was ever paid me by the Church or for any service as a minister of the Everlasting Gospel. I lost nearly all I had when we were broken up in Missouri and driven from that State; I was nearly stripped again when Joseph Smith was murdered and we were driven from Illinois; but nothing was ever made up to me by the Church, nor by any one. I believe I know how to acquire property and how to take care of it.

H.G.—Can you give me any rational explanation of the aversion and hatred with which your people are generally regarded by those among whom they have lived and with whom they have been brought directly in contact?

B.Y.—No other explanation than is afforded by the crucifixion of Christ and the kindred treatment of God's ministers, prophets and saints of all ages.

H.G.—I know that a new sect is always decried and traduced—that it is hardly ever deemed respectable to belong to one—that the Baptists, Quakers, Methodists, Universalists, &c., have each in their turn been regarded in the infancy of their sect as the offscouring of the earth; yet I cannot remember that either of them were ever generally represented and regarded by the older sects of their early days as thieves, robbers, murderers.

B.Y.—If you will consult the contemporary Jewish accounts of the life and acts of Jesus Christ, you will find that he and his disciples were accused of every abominable deed and purpose—robbery and murder included. Such a work is still extant and may be found by those who seek it.

H.G.—What do you say of the so-called Danites, or Destroying Angels, belonging to your Church?

B.Y.—What do *you* say? I know of no such band, no such persons or organizations. I hear of them only in the slanders of our enemies.

H.G.—With regard, then, to the grave question on which your doctrines and practices are avowedly at war with those of the Christian world— that of a plurality of wives—is the system of your Church acceptable to the majority of its women?

B.Y.—They could not be more averse to it than I was when it was first revealed to us as the Divine will. I think they generally accept it, as I do, as the will of God.

H.G.—How general is polygamy among you?

B.Y.—I could not say. Some of those present [heads of the Church] have each but one wife; others have more: each determines what is his individual duty.

H.G.—What is the largest number of wives belonging to any one man?

B.Y.—I have fifteen; I know no one who has more; but some of those sealed to me are old ladies whom I regard rather as mothers than wives, but whom I have taken home to cherish and support.

H.G.—Does not the Apostle Paul say that a bishop should be "the husband of one wife?"

B.Y.—So we hold. We do not regard any but a married man as fitted for the office of bishop. But the Apostle does not forbid a bishop having more wives than one.

H.G.—Does not Christ say that he who puts away his wife, or marries one whom another has put away, commits adultery?

B.Y.—Yes; and I hold that no man should ever put away a wife except for adultery—not always even for that. Such is *my* individual view of the matter. I do not say that wives have never been put away in our Church, but that I do not approve of the practice.

H.G.—How do you regard what is commonly termed the Christian Sabbath?

B.Y.—As a divinely appointed day of rest. We enjoin all to rest from secular labor on that day. We would have no man enslaved to the Sabbath, but we enjoin all to respect and enjoy it.

———————

—Such is, as nearly as I can recollect, the substance of nearly two hours'conversation, wherein much was said incidentally that would not be worth reporting, even if I could remember and reproduce it, and wherein others bore a part; but, as President Young is the first minister of the Mormon Church, and bore the principal part in the conversation, I have reported his answers alone to my questions and observations. The others appeared uniformly to defer to his views, and to acquiesce fully in his responses and explanations. He spoke readily, not always with grammatical accuracy, but with no appearance of hesitation or reserve, and with no apparent desire to conceal anything, nor did he repel any of my questions as impertinent. He was very plainly dressed in thin summer clothing, and with no air of sanctimony or fanaticism. In appearance, he is a portly, frank, good-natured, rather thick-set man of fifty-five, seeming to enjoy life, and be in no particular hurry to get to heaven. His associates are plain men, evidently born and reared to a life of labor, and looking as little like crafty hypocrites or swindlers as any body of men I ever met. The absence of cant or snuffle from their manner was marked and general, yet, I think I may fairly say that their Mormonism has not impoverished them—that they were generally poor men when they embraced it, and are now in very comfortable circumstances—as men averaging three or four wives apiece certainly need to be.

If I hazard any criticisms on Mormonism generally, I reserve them for a separate letter, being determined to make this a fair and full exposé of the doctrine and polity, in the very words of its Prophet, so far as I can recall them. I do not believe President Young himself could present them in terms calculated to render them less obnoxious to the Gentile world than the above. But I have a right to add here, because I said it to the assembled chiefs at the close of the above colloquy, that the degradation (or, if you please, the restriction) of Woman to the single office of child-bearing and its accessories, is an inevitable consequence of the system here paramount. I have not observed a sign in the streets, an advertisement in the journals, of this Mormon metropolis, whereby a woman proposes to do anything whatever. No Mormon has ever cited to me his wife's or any woman's opinion on any subject; no Mormon woman has been introduced or has spoken to me; and, though I have been asked to visit Mormons in their houses, no one has spoken of his wife (or wives) desiring to see me, or his desiring me to make her (or their) acquaintance, or voluntarily indicated the existence of such a being or beings. I will not attempt to report our talk on this subject, because, unlike what I have above given, it assumed somewhat the character of a disputation, and I could hardly give it impartially; but one remark made by President Young I think I can give accurately, and it may serve as a sample of all that was offered on that side. It was in these words, I think exactly: "If I did not consider myself competent to transact a certain business without taking my wife's or any woman's counsel with regard to it, I think I ought to let that business alone." The spirit with regard to Woman, of the entire Mormon, as of all other polygamic systems, is fairly displayed in this avowal. Let any such system become established and prevalent, and Woman will soon be confined to the harem, and her appearance in the street with unveiled face will be accounted immodest. I joyfully trust that the genius of the Nineteenth Century tends to a solution of the problem of Woman's sphere and destiny radically different from this.

H. G.

Polygamy, Politics and the Union Pacific Railroad

Ohio State Journal, November 6, 1882

The Mormons, doubtless encouraged thereto by expected Democratic victories, are growing bolder and more outspoken in regard to their peculiar institution. Hon. George Q. Cannon, an ex-Congressional delegate, and one of the Twelve apostles of the Mormon Church, is making speeches in advocacy of polygamy, and blaming the non-polygamic Mormons with being the immediate cause of all the trouble which has come upon the church. He admonishes the brothers and sisters who are not living in polygamy that they are not to be "the saviors of the Latter

day saints." "If this people are saved it will be through the men and
women who have obeyed this divine command, and this is as true as if
spoken by any angel from heaven." The logical sequence of such a creed
is followed up in this manner: "If we cannot obey the laws of our country and God, better far for us to obey God. Let us go from this Conference and obey the revelations we have heard better than we have heretofore."

By the "laws of our country" Apostle Cannon of the course alludes
more particularly to the Edmunds law, which is now being put in force
in Utah, and by "the revelations" he means the injunction to practice
polygamy.

But Mr. Cannon goes further still in his defiance and tells his followers that "if we had obeyed the counsels of the prophets of God we would
have kept these people from getting a foothold here. We have warmed a
viper in our bosom, and it has stung us," and in this he doubtless has reference to the customs of the Mormons, in the days before the completion
of the Pacific railroad, when Gentiles were fewer, and communication
with the United States much less expeditious than now. In those palmy
days the "avengers of blood" could very easily rid the community of an
obnoxious interloper, and no questions were asked. The brutal murder of
Dr. Robinson in the streets of Salt Lake City, and the Mountain Meadow
massacre, were illustrations of how the church attempted to prevent the
vipers from getting a foothold there.

And this horrible, unrepublican system is now more active in its pro-
pagandism than ever before. Its emissaries are scouring the countries of
Europe and the remote portions of our Southern States, openly recruiting
for their infernal purposes, and defying every law, human and divine,
while the United States Commission is in Utah endeavoring to enforce
laws which shall put a stop to the system.

In 1867, when Mr. Sam. Bowles wrote that the extension of the Pacific railroad through Salt Lake City would be the solution of the Mormon question, he little appreciated the devotion of that people to their
system, and the skill of the Mormon leaders in taking advantage of the
new relations which the railroad would place them in toward the Gentile
world. Brigham Young had the sagacity to make the best of the situation,
and to control it for his own purposes. He took the contract to build the
railroad in his Territory, and himself built the branch from the main line
at Ogden to Salt Lake City, making a large profit in the operation.
Bishop Sharp, a Mormon official, has been a Director in the Union Pa-

cific road ever since it was built, and has been shrewd enough to make a great deal of money out of its securities. The completed road offered increased facilities to bring recruits from distant lands, and the growth of the church from immigration has been greater than ever before. The audacity of that people would seem to be so rapidly growing that Congress will be driven to such extreme measures as will put an effectual quietus on their operations.

10

A Nation Divided

From the very beginning, the institution of slavery presented Americans with a dilemma that was both religious and political. As a religious question, divergent views, all firmly rooted in the Bible, provided the moral underpinnings both for those who supported slavery and those who opposed it. As a political question, it provided a focus for diverse views about the scope and meaning of the freedom for which people fought and died in the Revolutionary War. At the same time, slavery also raised serious constitutional questions about the authority of the federal government and the meaning of states' rights.

All of those concerns came to the fore and intermingled with each other and with more mundane considerations of economic and regional self-interest as the young nation grappled first with terms for admitting western territories into the union and then with the Civil War itself. The articles reproduced in this chapter illustrate the ways in which religious and political beliefs intertwined with purely pragmatic concerns to shape views on slavery, abolition and the Civil War.

The "Petition from Baptists in Missouri Concerning Slavery and Statehood" is a typical remonstrance arguing against slavery, yet opposing federal intervention in that question on constitutional grounds. "Mr. Douglas on the Preachers" begins with a remonstrance sent to Congress by New England clergy who argue that slavery is wrong on moral grounds. However, the Mormon-owned *Deseret News,* from which the version in this chapter is taken, coupled that protest with an attack on clergy meddling. The themes of northern duplicity and hypocrisy in that attack figure even more prominently in news coverage from southern papers and from the Copperhead press in the North.

Both "Praying for the Union" and "Morals of the North" ran in the *Charleston Mercury,* but "Praying for the Union" first appeared in the *New York Herald.* Although Bennett generally sided with the underdog, he consistently opposed abolition and the Civil War, at least partly out of concern that cheap labor from freed slaves would undermine the already precarious economic position of Irish Catholic immigrants. As early as September 11, 1835, Bennett published commentary critical of abolitionists. On March 21, 1854, the *Herald* attacked the well-known antislavery clergyman, Henry Ward Beecher, for delivering from the pulpit a political speech opposing the Nebraska Bill that Bennett supported; seven days later Bennett produced an essay likening abolitionists to the Native American Party.

"Morals of the North" is typical of Southerners' states' rights beliefs. Like Bennett's commentary, it also portrays Northerners as opportunistic and hypocritical meddlers. But however much Southerners may have condemned their foes for enlisting God in their cause, they also turned to God for support. As secession led inevitably to war, prayers and sermons supporting the cause became increasingly common features in southern newspapers. A typical sermon can be found in the *Charleston Mercury* on December 14, 1860.

Perhaps the most influential paper in support of the northern cause was the *New-York Daily Tribune*. Horace Greeley's concerns about slavery can be seen in the questions he asked Brigham Young in the interview reproduced in chapter 9. In January and February of 1854, Greeley published important exchanges between the Rev. Henry Ward Beecher and his critics. As an open letter to President Abraham Lincoln, Greeley's "Prayer of Twenty Million," published in the *Tribune* on August 20, 1862, both reflected and helped shape northern opinion. Lincoln's reply to that impassioned argument for emancipation, along with Greeley's response to Lincoln's reply, can be found in the paper on August 25. However, in contrast to those religio-political items, the "Church and State" column reproduced in this chapter speaks to the divisive effects of arguments over slavery and the Civil War on the churches. As a roundup of church news, it illustrates the use of religious publications as news sources.

A Petition from Baptists in Missouri Concerning Slavery and Statehood

Niles' Register, November 27, 1819

From the *Missouri Intelligencer*

To the senate and house of representatives of the United States of America, in congress assembled.

The delegates from the several baptist churches of CHRIST, composing the Mount Pleasant association, holden at *Mount Zion* meeting-house, Howard county, and territory of Missouri, on the 11th, 12th and 13th days of September, in the year of our Lord one thousand eight hundred and nineteen,—having finished the business for which they convened together, and viewing with deep concern the present situation of our beloved country,—take the opportunity, being thus assembled, to declare;—

That, as a people, the *baptists* have always been republican, they have been among the first to mark, and to raise their voice against oppression, and ever ready to defend their rights, with their fortunes and their lives: in this they are supported as well by the principles which organized the revolution, and secured our independence as a nation, as by those recognized in our bill of rights, and that constitution which as citizens we are bound to support.

Viewing the constitution of the United States, as the result of the *united* experience of statesmen and patriots of the revolution, and as the sacred palladium of our religious as well as civil liberty, we cannot without the most awful apprehension look on any attempt to violate its provisions, and believing that the vote of a majority of the last congress, restricting the good people of this territory in the formation of their constitution for a state government to be in direct opposition thereto; we would enter our most solemn protest against the principles endeavored to be supported thereby. Because, our government is a solemn covenant entered into between the citizens of the United States, pledging our fortunes, our persons, and our lives, to defend and protect to each other, the enjoyment of the privileges intended to be secured; and altho' with *Washington, Jefferson,* and every other person, we regret the existence of slavery at all, and altho' we feel it our duty to alleviate the situation of the unfortunate beings who are its subjects among us, and anxiously look forward to the time when a happy emancipation can be effected consistent with principles of safety and *justice*—

Yet, we believe that "the powers not delegated to the United States by the constitution, nor prohibited by it to the states, are reserved to the states respectively, or to the people."

By the treaty of cession, "The inhabitants of the ceded territory, shall be incorporated in the union of the United States, and admitted as soon as possible, according to the principles of the federal constitution, to the enjoyment of *all* the rights, advantages, and immunities of citizens of the United States; and in the mean time they shall be maintained and protected in the free enjoyment of their liberty, property, and the religion which they profess."

The 3d sec. of the 4th article of the constitution provides that, "No person held to service or labor in one state under the laws thereof, escaping into another, shall, in consequence of any law or regulation therein, be discharged from such service or labor, but shall be delivered up, on claim of the party to whom such service of labor may be due."

The necessity of these provisions grew out of the political situation of the states forming the constitutions, as explained in the words of our beloved Washington, in his letter to the president of the congress.

The constitution does not admit slaves to be freemen; it does admit them to become *property,* and guarantees to the master an ownership, which his fellow-citizens, living in another state holding other principles, cannot legislate from him: and as under the constitution, a sister state cannot emancipate those slaves who flee to its jurisdiction, and as the power is not expressly delegated to congress, they cannot emancipate a slave, for the right is reserved to the people.—And if they cannot emancipate a slave in a state, and it be lawful to hold slaves in this territory, congress neither have the right to emancipate our slaves whilst we live in a territorial form, nor under a state government; for, by the treaty of cession, congress are not only bound to admit us into the union, but are bound to protect us in the free enjoyment of our liberty and property—and therefore, not only our right to admission into the union, but our right to hold slaves is secured by the treaty of cession, which is ratified by the president and senate, and also by several acts of congress.

With awful apprehensions we view the principle involved in this question; we are bound to hope that many are conscientious in endeavoring to enforce the proposed restriction—and we believe that they are carried away by a blind zeal and mistaken philanthropy, with due deference we would ask, if the same *zeal* that would trample on the said provisions of the constitution to emancipate a slave, if actuated by ignorance and prejudice, and stimulated by policy, would not violate a provision still more dear to us as Christians. To enslave the conscience in the establishment of a religion—from the violation of the sacred rights of property, and the still more sacred rights of conscience is but one step. Witness the attempt made in Virginia, the birth place of *Washington.*

Relying on the wisdom of God, we hail with Christian gratitude those manifestations of his providence, which tend to lessen the burden imposed on the unfortunate slaves, and hope that not only we, but all who profess the religion of *Jesus* will always aid any measures tending thereto. And believing that the policy proposed in the restriction will not only cause jealousy, foment discord, and shake the foundation of our government, but by confining them to one small district, will increase the task, augment the pains and rivet the chains of the slaves, we warn you in the name of humanity itself to beware.

The time has arrived when it is possible to admit us into the union—we have all the means necessary for a state government. And believing that the question of slavery is one which belongs exclusively to the state to decide on, we, on behalf of ourselves, our fellow citizens, and of the most solemn faith of the nation, claim admission into the union on the principles of the *federal constitution*—on an equal footing with the other states.

Praying that God, who grants so many blessings to us as a nation, to guide and direct you not only in this, but in other questions; that he will make you wise to the preservation of all our rights, with the most sincere and ardent attachment to the principles of our government, we subscribe ourselves your fellow citizens.

Signed by order and on behalf of the association.

EDWARD TURNER, *Moderator.*

Geo. Stapleton, clerk.

Mr. Douglas on the Preachers

Deseret News, May 24, 1854

Our readers have been advised that the Ministers of New England, sent a protest against the Nebraska Bill to the Senate. Mr. Everett presented it. It was in the following words:

> *To the honorable the Senate and House of Representatives of the United States in Congress assembled.*

The undersigned clergymen of different denominations, in New England, hereby, in the name of Almighty God, and in his presence, do solemnly protest against the passage of what is known as Nebraska bill, or any repeal or modification of the existing legal prohibitions against slavery in that part of our national domain which it is proposed to organize into the territories of Nebraska and Kansas. We protest against it as a great moral wrong—as a breach of faith eminently injurious to the moral principles of the community, and subversive of all confidence in national engagements—as a measure full of danger to the peace, and even existence of our beloved Union, and exposing us to the righteous judgments of the Almighty—and your protestants as in duty bound, will ever pray.

Dated at Boston, this 1st day of March, A.D., 1854.

Mr Douglas arose as soon as the memorial was read, and immediately pitched into the preachers—Among other things, he said:

"It protests against our action as being a breach of faith, as involving a moral wrong, as destructive of all confidence, and as subjecting us to the righteous judgment of the Almighty. It is presented, too, by a denomination of men calling themselves preachers of the gospel. It has been demonstrated in debate that there is not a particle of truth in the allegation of a breach of faith or breach of confidence—It has been demonstrated so clearly that there is no excuse for any man in the community who believes it any longer. Yet here we find a large body of preachers, perhaps three thousand, following the lead of a circular which was calculated to mislead and deceive the public. They have here come forward with an atrocious falsehood and an atrocious calumny against this body, and prostituted the pulpit, prostituted the sacred desk to the miserable and corrupting influence of party politics.—[Ex.]

Praying for the Union

Charleston Mercury, December 20, 1860

The efficacy of prayer has been admitted by so many generations and in so many different creeds that it would be a work of supererogation to deny it at this late day. It is, however, a curious fact that the cruelty of a nation increases in the exact ratio of its piety. Probably the hardest praying people that the world has ever seen are the Hindoo Brahmins and the Arab Sheiks. The time which they do not occupy in their devotions, or in the ordinary affairs of every day life, is taken up for the devising of plans for the cutting off of heretics and infidels. When the Spanish inquisitors put a poor trembling wretch upon the rack, *aves* and *paters* without number were thrown in free of charge. That Queen of England known as "Bloody Mary" was rarely away from her oratory, and James the Second was as pious as he was mean, which is saying a great deal. Nor were the Dissenters much better. Cromwell never prayed that the hearts of the cavaliers might be turned from the error of their ways, but he asked that the arms of the Covenanters might be strengthened so that they could smite the friends of the man Stuart, even as the children of Israel overthrew the Midianites.

This fanatical spirit seems to have been transmitted in the blood of the Puritans, and disseminated throughout New England and some parts of the North. With a few honorable exceptions the Northern clergy has labored zealously to draw down Divine vengeance on the South. In every New England village sermons have been preached against the "sins" of the South. Without doubt this this [sic] tendency of the pulpit has aided greatly in the abolitionizing of the North. The people of New England are naturally a pious, God-fearing, praying and preaching race. They have, both in State and Church, a bad way of jumping at the conclusion that they are right, and every body else necessarially wrong; and, therefore we are not surprised to find them in the attitude of utter hostility to the South.—*N.Y. Herald.*

Morals of the North

Charleston Mercury, December 29, 1860

Our beloved brethren of the North, the men of ideas and philanthropy, and virtuous abstractions, have but one great grief in this Confederacy—that their consciences suffer because of the degree of responsibility which is theirs, as connected with a Confederacy in which slavery exists. One would think that a short process could be found by which to relieve their consciences of this dreadful moral responsibility—simply by quitting the connection. But the hypocrisy exposes itself the moment the Slave States propose to relieve them by their own withdrawal from the Union. And then they ignore their own peace and philanthropy doctrines by insisting upon carrying war and carnage into the South, to compel the continuance of that very Union which was their loathing and horror. Mr. LINCOLN and the Union savers all, allege that they have no design against the peace, the safety, or the institutions of the South; and all they ask of the South is, simply, that they should have a trial, only to prove how innocent they are. Excellent Christians! Admirable politicians! Virtuous philanthropists! They curse slavery, threaten its destruction, and use all their energies to acquire the power to destroy it. And when they

think they have got this power and are exulting in it, they suddenly ab-
jure it. The victim struggles. They did not think that—for hypocrites are
always fools as well as knaves. He may free himself, perhaps, before his
throat is cut. If we now can only persuade him to be quiet! There's the
rub! Who shall we look to? DOUGLAS CRITTENEEN, WINTER
DAVIS, BOTTS—by, BOTTS!

These tender consciences should be relieved from the moral hurt
which they suffer from connection with Slave States.

We quit them accordingly. We release them.

These world-wide philanthropists, peace men and innocents, repudiate
war, and strife, and all bad passions.

We propose to quit them in peace, after a fashion prescribed in the
Scriptures—"You go your ways; we go ours."

Why will these Innocents, who loath the Union with the slaveholder,
still insist upon it, even at the risk of war? Alas, brethren! They wish,
themselves, to become slaveholders; not of the negro, but the white races
of the South! They have long since cheated brother ESAU, who was a
simple herdsman, of his mess of pottage. They would now sell him into
Egypt, and reduce him to brick-making, without straw, that they should
build themselves mighty pyramids. Their weapons will not prevail. But
what a fearful power have they in their cunning! How dextrously do they
mask their faces with ESAU'S hair, and approaching our poor benighted
brethren, the Patriarchs, BELL and CRITTENDEN, and others, persuade
the poor blind men that they are the favorite brothers, the best friends,
the true heirs; while, with cormorant appetites, they devour the pottage;
and, with irreverent scorn, they mock the blessing. But the great God of
the world still governs it; and His eyes are not blind to the acts of the
wicked. In His own good time, He will rebuke the cunning hypocrites;
the pottage shall be as poison in their throats and bowels; and the blessing shall become the curse.

Church and State

New-York Daily Tribune, August 23, 1862

—The boldest encroachments ever attempted by the Pro-Slavery
Churches of the South upon the territory of the Free States of the Union
was the organization of congregations and conferences of the Methodist

Episcopal Church South in California and Oregon. Each church, school, paper and member of these conferences was an agent for preparing the way for the introduction of Slavery into these States. It is one of the many blessings of this war that the Methodist Episcopal Church South in the two Pacific States is now threatened with extinction. The many and persevering efforts which have been made to establish it upon a permanent basis have all failed. Dr. Jesse Boring, the first founder of Southern Methodist congregations on the Pacific, spent some $20,000 of his private funds on account of his church in San Francisco, and was never reimbursed. Some five years since, the Southern Conference resumed the work, as they thought under better auspices. A new paper was started, a metropolitan church edifice was projected for San Francisco, to cost some forty or fifty thousand dollars; a book depository was established, Oregon was occupied, a college enterprise was started, and all departments of the work of building up the denomination were pushed with vigor approaching desperation. But what has been the result? The paper suspended some months since, the editor having worked three years without salary, and expended $6,000 of his private funds to keep it afloat. The book depository is about to close, with no purpose of attempting to reopen it. The college is no more than a small preparatory school. In Oregon, the race of the church is nearly run. In short, the cause of Southern Methodism on the Pacific Coast is generally collapsed, and will soon cease to exist.

—The American war will furnish some additional material for the science of canonical law. Two disloyal members of the Second Presbyterian Church of Nashville having usurped the control of the church edifice and parsonage, and ousted the loyal pastor thereof, the United States military authorities at Nashville have restored the church to the direction and control of the loyal portion of the congregation.

—One of the foremost theological scholars of the slave power, Dr. Thomwell, died at Charlotte, N.C., Aug. 8. He was until the outbreak of the Rebellion one of the leading men of the Old School Presbyterian Church, and few men have done more than he to pervert the views of the Southern churches respecting Slavery.

—Nearly all the freedmen of South Carolina are under the ministration of Baptist missionaries, who derive their support from the American Baptist Home Missionary and the American Baptist Publication Societies. The missionaries are active and efficient, and speak encouragingly of the progress of their labors. Large numbers of the colored population have been baptised, after giving satisfactory evidence of their religious condition.

—*The Southern Lutheran,* in Charleston, S.C., a rabid Secession sheet, publishes the following sentiment by the Rev. Dr. Bachman, one of the most aged clergymen of Charleston, and author of a book on the Unity of the Human Race, in which he maintained that negroes are human beings, and descended from Adam:

"You may fetter the arms and bind a freeman in chains—you may lay him in a dungeon, and place a gag in his mouth, *but the moment he breaks his shackles, he will rise up a man,* AND THEN WO[E] TO HIS OPPRESSORS."

Of course, in the opinion of the author, this is meant only for the benefit of the white Secessionists; but if the slaveholders should ever allow their slaves to learn how to read, sentences like the above might teach the slaves a very dangerous lesson.

—The editor of *The Central Christian Advocate* of St. Louis has learned from Col. Bussey that two of the three missionaries of the Methodist Episcopal Church in Arkansas have been murdered, and that the church herself is now extinct. The editor thinks that little or nothing can be done in that State for several years, and that it will take one or two generations to replant it in that region.

—It seems that the military laws of Ohio do not exempt ministers from drafting. *The Evangelical Messenger,* of Dayton, O., thinks that ministers of the gospel must go as substitutes for the negroes whom the Government refuses to accept.

—The Rev. J.B. Himes, who has so many times fixed upon the year in which this present world is to come to an end, is starting out on a new mission to give himself "entirely to the work of preaching these things"—the coming of the Lord in 1867 or 1868.

—The French Court of Perigneux has recently decided the great question of the marriage of priests. An ex-priest, Mr. Bron de Lauriores, has, in spite of the doctrine of the Catholic Church, that holy orders are indelible, professed to throw them off and claim the right of contracting a civil marriage. Whether such marriage can be legally contracted in France, has been long a controverted point, and from several decisions like that of the Court of Cassation in 1833, it became the habit to refuse marriage to persons renouncing the priesthood. It was, however, only a habit, for there is nothing in the French laws which says that it ought to be so. This is what the decision at Perigneux has admitted, and it has done so with a clearness of views which can leave no doubt on the subject.

—Alarming revelations are made on the increase of suicides in France. In the space of thirty-two years from 1827 to 1858 inclusively, 92,622 suicides were committed in France, being an average of 2,895 in the year. The suicides of males, which have only been kept distinct since 1836, amount to 56,562, and of females to 18,548—the yearly average for the former being 2,450 and for the latter 807. The difference is only to be explained by the fact that the religious sentiment sets more powerfully on women than on men. It is proved by the official returns that the most religious provinces present the fewest suicides, and that the proportion of suicides increases as we approach Paris, where it attains the maximum. Old age even does not seem to allay the furore for self-destruction: the proportion constantly increases from childhood to the age of eighty when it begins to decline.

—The agitation in Switzerland against the emancipation of the Jews seems to be successful. In the canton of Aurgan, which is the only one that has a Jewish population of any amount, the people have been called upon to vote on the dissolution of the Grand Council (the House of Representatives,) which had decreed the emancipation, and has decided by 25,000 votes against 16,000 in favor of the dissolution. As the law of emancipation was the only ostensible reason for which the dissolution of the Grand Council was demanded, the repeal of the law by a new Grand Council seems to be certain.

11

The "Jesus Newspaper"

By the end of the 19th century, newspapers had come to rely on professional reporters to gather local news and the telegraph to transmit it from the scene of action to papers around the world. They began to emphasize the new and unusual. Many papers adopted or adapted the news formulas of the "yellow press." To compete with each other and satisfy public demand for news, they published on Sunday in spite of blue laws and clergy protests. Although those changes were generally popular, they also raised questions about the influence of the "yellow press" and the proper practice of journalism.

In that climate, the Rev. Charles E. Sheldon, clergy author of the still-popular *In His Steps,* proposed a plan to protect public morals and improve the practice of journalism by creating a daily newspaper edited the way Jesus would edit it. In response, the *Topeka Daily Capital* gave him complete editorial control of the paper for one week, March 13–19, 1900.

Sheldon accepted the offer and the *Capital* announced the experiment with great fanfare on January 23, with a front page devoted entirely to hyping Sheldon and the "Jesus Newspaper." "Unique Idea in the History of Journalism" provides the background for the experiment. "The Topeka *Capital* This Week," taken from the first Sheldon edition, describes Sheldon's press philosophy; "The Saturday Evening Edition" tells of Sheldon's plan to replace the Sunday paper with an extra Saturday edition devoted to material "suitable for Sunday reading."

Newspapers around the country and the fledgling *Associated Press* commented on the experiment and reported its progress. Subscriptions poured in. The March 11 *Daily Capital* reported:

> The subscription list to the Capital for Sheldon week yesterday passed the 300,000 mark. The subscriptions have come from forty-eight states and twenty-seven foreign countries . . .

On March 17, the ever-skeptical *Atchinson Daily Globe* reported:

> The Sheldon edition of the Topeka Capital has grown to such size that it has been necessary to arrange for its publication in New York, Chicago and Kansas City as well as in Topeka.

But the *Globe* also noted dissatisfaction among regular subscribers and advertisers and delightedly took potshots at Sheldon's refusal to carry ads for corsets, patent medicines and "secret societies," as well as at the paper's lack of "telegraphic dispatches" and real local news. During the first four days of the experiment, the *Globe* published these irreverent comments as the one-line quotes under its masthead:

> Children Soon Learn That On Nights When They Forget To Say Their Prayers, Nothing Terrible Happens.

> If You Do Not Practice Honesty, Justice, Truth and Industry, the Church Cannot Keep You Out of Hell.

> The Men Guilty of the Hold-Ups in Kansas City, Should Know That During Lent, Their Conduct Is Improper.

> The Women's Sign of Spring, the Violet, Is Not Here, but the Men's Favorite Sign Is: Bock Beer.

On March 17, "The Disciples of Brer. Sheldon Are Now Engaged in a Row That Will Add to the General Merriment" appeared under the masthead. As the top story, the *Globe* published the *Associated Press* account, which is included in this chapter, of dissension at the *Capital* under the headline "The Devil at Topeka."

In spite of its popularity, ultimately most observers concluded the "Jesus Newspaper" had failed as journalism. In "The Sheldon Edition of the Capital," reproduced in this chapter, the editor, who had never endorsed Sheldon's experiment, reflects on lessons learned from the experiment and offers thoughtful commentary on the proper role for religious publications and publications intended for a mass audience. From March 20 through March 25, the paper published both favorable and unfavorable comments about the experiment from clergy and newspapers including the *Chicago Tribune, Commercial-Appeal, Kansas City Star, New York Times* and the *New York World.*

Unique Idea in the History of Journalism

Its Birth and Development Into a Far-Reaching Plan to Elevate the Press

The Topeka Daily Capital, January 23, 1900

THE CAPITAL this morning makes an announcement that is unique in the history of journalism. Rev. Charles M. Sheldon, author of "In His Steps," will, on March 13 next, assume the entire editorial and business control of this paper. For six days he will be its absolute owner. Unhampered, he will dictate its policy; edit its news columns; control its advertising. In a word, he will embody his idea of what a Christian daily newspaper should be.

CRADLED AT DETROIT IN JULY

This conception was cradled at Detroit last July. It took form in a query which startled one of the largest assemblies of Christian workers ever gathered. Mr. Sheldon asked this question, "In this day, when philanthropy munificently endows our institutions of learning, is there here a man who, recognizing the potency of the public press to make or mar our civilization, will contribute a million dollars to establish a daily Christian newspaper?"

ITS SIGNIFICANCE AND GROWTH

The significance of this suggestion received instant and widespread recognition. It went at once from the great Christian Endeavor convention, in which it was uttered, to the world.

Why?

The press is the vanguard of civilization. The daily paper is its vitality.

This is an age of government by newspaper.

The press convenes law-making bodies, marshals armies, builds navies. It declares wars and dictates the terms of peace. It is the die in which opinion is cast. It is the force which makes opinion effective.

GIVING EFFECT TO THE PLAN

Responding to the interest aroused by what has come to be known as the Sheldon idea, the Topeka Daily Capital, a modern daily newspaper, the leading journal of dignity and importance of the state in which Mr. Sheldon resides; equipped with every mechanical facility to give effect to the plan, made tender of its plant, franchises, contracts and property to the experiment. With a deep appreciation of all that is involved, it is prepared to abdicate its news, editorial and business interests to Mr. Sheldon and his aides, that he may demonstrate his idea of the needed reform in the daily press by tendering to the country an example of a Christian daily newspaper. Accompanying it is a realization of what may be the tremendous significance of a reform in this respect. Sheldon's idea is charged with prodigious possibilities. It may inject the Christianizing ethics of a higher civilization into the coming generation. It may put a new complexion of morality, thought and human conduct upon the growing age. Its ramifications may be infinite.

Mr. Sheldon himself fully realizes the gravity of the trust he has assumed and is content reverently to make himself the conspicuous mark of this effort.

He will call to his assistance the best minds and the best exemplars of modern Christian thought, and, confident of the far-reaching effect of what he may accomplish, the Topeka Capital commits the Sheldon idea to the considerate judgment of all mankind.

The Topeka *Capital* This Week

The Topeka Daily Capital, March 13, 1900

Last December the owners of the Topeka Daily Capital asked me to assume entire charge of the paper for one week and edit it as a distinctly Christian daily.

I have accepted the invitation on condition that I receive no financial compensation and that a share of the profits be used for some benevolent work, and named the week beginning Tuesday, March 13, 1900, as the week for the experiment. With the hearty co-operation of every person connected with the paper and with the help of the wisdom that I have prayed might be given me from Him who is wiser than any of us, I shall do the best I can.

If a thousand different Christian men who wished to edit Christian dailies should make an honest attempt to do so, the result might be a thousand different papers in very many particulars. In other words, these Christian editors might arrive at different conclusions in the interpretation of what is Christian. It is, of course, the farthest from my purpose to attempt to show in a dogmatic way what is the one thing that Jesus would do in every case. The only thing I or any other Christian man can do in the interpretation of what is Christian in the conduct of this paper is to define the term Christian the best that can be done after asking for divine wisdom, and not judge others who might with equal desire and sincerity interpret the probable action of Jesus in a different manner.

With this understanding of the conduct of the paper this week, I will state in part its general purpose and policy.

1. It will be a news paper. The word "news" will be defined as anything in the way of daily events that the public ought to know for its development and power in a life of righteousness. Of necessity the editor of this paper, or of any other with this definition of "news," will determine not only the kind, but the quantity of any particular events that ought to be printed. The importance of one kind of "news" compared with another kind will also determine the place in the paper where matter will be printed. If it seems to the editor that certain subjects representing great causes that belong to the profoundest principles of human life are the most important, they will be given the first page of the paper whether they are telegraphic items or not. It might easily become the settled policy of a permanent paper similar to this one, to consider the detailed account of an unusual battle as of less importance to the reader than an account of the usual daily destruction being caused by liquor. The first page of the Capital this week will contain what seems to the editor to be the most vital issues that affect humanity as a whole.

2. The paper will be non-partisan, not only in municipal and state politics, but also in national politics. I do not mean to say that a Christian daily can not be partisan. This is simply my interpretation of Christian as applied to this part of the paper's life.

3. On the liquor question the paper will advocate the prohibition of the whole liquor business from Maine to California and all around the globe. By prohibition I mean the total extinction of the curse of making, selling, buying and drinking intoxicating liquor; its extinction by legal enactment, by personal total abstinence, and by every form of state, home, church and school education that Christians can devise.

4. The great social questions of the age will be given prominance. The selfishness of mankind in every form of greed, commercially or politically, will be considered as of more serious consequences to us as a people than many other matters which too often engage the time and attention of mankind.

5. The paper will declare its abhorrence of war as it is being waged today not only in Africa but in the Philippines and everywhere else.

6. On matters of "finance" or "tariff" or "expansion," matters of public concern which have to do with measures of this character, the editor has personal opinions which may or may not be voiced in this paper. If he gives expression to them it will be in no dogmatic or positive manner, as if he knew what the whole Christian truth was concerning them. In regard to many of these questions I do not know what is the Christian answer to them. In regard to others, my study of them has not yet resulted in convictions that are strong enough to print. I do not wish to declare through this paper a policy concerning certain political measures which are not clear in my own mind.

7. The main purpose of the paper will be to influence its readers to seek first the Kingdom of God. A nation seeking the Kingdom of God first of all, will in time find right answers to all disputed questions and become a powerful and useful nation.

8. Editorial, and other articles, written by reporters, will be signed by the writers. The exceptions will be small items and such local and telegraphic news as in its nature does not require signature.

9. There will be no Sunday paper, but instead a Saturday evening edition suitable for Sunday reading.

I wish to take this opportunity to thank the many friends everywhere who have sent me words of encouragement. It has been impossible for me to answer them personally. I also wish to express to the host of Christian correspondents who have sent me assurances of their prayers for this week's work, my deep acknowledgement of the source of whatever strength I have felt in preparing for a task which lies beyond the reach of any merely human effort.

May God bless the use of this paper to the glory of His Kingdom on the earth.

CHARLES M. SHELDON

The Saturday Evening Edition

The Topeka Daily Capital, March 17, 1900

We read in the Bible that God rested after the work of the creation, then declared that this rest period was to be observed by the human race.

The great wisdom of this divine command has never been questioned by the most thoughtful men and women. The reasons why we need a regular, recurring period of rest for body and mind are so many and so sensible that they are practically self evident. Disobedience to the command has always resulted in loss to nations and individuals. Obedience to it has always resulted in blessing to nations and individuals.

It is with a very profound belief in the value of this one day out of seven that this particular issue of the Capital has been published. One of the greatest blessings connected with Sunday ought to be the opportunity it affords for a change of thought and a rest for mind and soul. On this account there is no news of the world published in this issue. The human race can be just as happy and useful and powerful it it does not know every twenty-four hours the news of the wars and the sports and the society events of the world. Let us give God a fair opportunity to reach our souls by turning from the six days of our earthly struggles which we call history, and letting our religious natures have a whole day in which to grow and express themselves. For we are religious before we are intellectual or artistic. Our souls are of more importance than our bodies. Let us give one whole day to God and to heaven, and to our Christian relations to our neighbor. We shall not lose anything if we do not know until Monday or even the next day what the world has been doing. It is not fair to shut out of our lives so much Him who made us to live to His glory on earth.

It is entirely possible for Christian civilization to be a great deal more powerful, useful and intelligent, if every one would take one whole day in seven to read what he does not read the other days of the week, to think what he does not think during the week, to rest, and pray, and commune with God, as he does not during the week. We have too much humanity if that is all we are willing to have. We need more divinity to make our lives complete.

It is hardly necessary for me to say that this particular kind of a paper for Sunday use might be varied in such a way as to bring to its readers each Saturday night a quantity of reading matter of great value. I have used the Bible for this one issue as an illustration of what might be done for every week in the year. I would have a different paper each time. The one thing kept in view each time would be to give the public something entirely different from the other issues of the paper. The editor of a daily paper ought not to be afraid to give the readers one paper during the week that would be distinctly religious. A special editor to take charge of this one number could find plenty of good material for the fifty-two weeks in the year and the amount of good that might be done by that last issue of each week is incalculable. The same plan could be pursued with an evening as with a morning paper. It would, however, be easier to do this with an evening instead of a morning paper. On that account if I were in charge of a Christian daily of my own I would choose an evening paper.

There has been no Sunday work done on this paper. The press and mailing work stopped before midnight of Saturday. The carriers were instructed to deliver their papers in time to reach home themselves before Sunday. There will be no papers sold or delivered on Sunday with the approval of the editor.

May God bless the use of the press of the world to the glory of His Kingdom on earth.

CHARLES M. SHELDON

The Devil at Topeka

Owners of the Capital Newspaper in a Row, With Brer. Sheldon Against Joe Hudson

Atchinson Globe, March 17, 1900

By *Associated Press*

TOPEKA, March 17—The *Capital* management is in a tremendous row over the future conduct of the paper. The directors are now holding an excited meeting. Popenoe, who favors its continuation as a religious daily, seems to have a majority of the directors in his favor. J. K. Hudson, the editor, and Dell Kizer, the business manager, strongly oppose the proposed idea. Mr. Hudson says emphatically he will not consent to run anything but a secular partisan newspaper. Mr. Kizer threatens suit against Popenoe for announcing a change of policy.

Dell Keiser, a director in the Topeka *Capital* company, president and business manager of the paper, announced to-day that the paper will not be continued according to Mr. Sheldon's plan. He says he will prevent the continuation of the venture by legal proceedings if necessary.

General J. K. Hudson, the editor in chief, announces that he will not be editor of anything but a secular partisan newspaper.

"I have never been in sympathy with the idea of a religious daily newspaper," said Gen. Hudson to-day. "There has been no secret about this. A year ago I said so editorially, and recently have said so to Mr. Sheldon and in interviews. I don't believe such a paper as Mr. Sheldon has made the *Capital* this week fills the bill of this day and age. What the present demands is a newspaper that gives all the news every day in the week, and reaches sinners as well as saints. The editorial page of a daily newspaper may be whatever the people in charge desire to make it, but the news columns should be devoted to the news of the world.

"I could no more edit a Christian newspaper than I could edit a populist or Democratic newspaper. It would be hypocrisy for me to attempt to edit such a paper as Mr. Sheldon has made the *Capital,* the same as it would be hypocrisy for me to attempt to edit the Kansas City *Times* along the principles it now advocates. I have my ideas as to what a daily newspaper should be, and I am too old to change them."

Hudson has a contract, with a number of years to run, as editor-in-chief in charge of the editorial policy of the *Capital* at a salary of three thousand dollars a year.

There is little joy in the Topeka *Capital* office. A Chicago *Record* dispatch from Topeka says: "Dell Keiser, the business manager, for the first time since Sheldon took hold, realized to-day that the real trouble would begin after the preacher had yielded his editorial chair. General Hudson, editor-in-chief, who was never in favor of the induction of Sheldon or his methods, said to-night that he was more than ever convinced of the futility of the Christian daily run as Jesus would run it, and he gave it as his opinion that, except from a financial standpoint, the thing was a failure. Even the money gain may be wiped out if the discarded advertisers choose to make their experience basis for suits at law. The fraternal organizations, many of whose "ads" were repudiated by Editor Sheldon, are very angry, and foreigners who did not like his attack this morning upon the methods and morals of the Bohemians, are asking what has become of Editor Sheldon's announcement that he would attack no race and no creed, but would deal as kindly with all people as he expected them to deal kindly with him.". . . F.O. Popenoe, principal owner of the Topeka *Capital,* announced last night that the *Capital* would continue as a Christian daily "indefinitely." This decision was arrived at after a conference between the *Capital* owners and Mr. Sheldon. Mr Sheldon gave it as his opinion that the paper could acquire a circulation of 100,000 if run on the Christian plan. The management will modify the Sheldon policy somewhat by printing more or less current news. All details concerning the future policy of the paper will be determined at a conference Monday afternoon. Mr. Sheldon will not remain in charge of the paper. His services could not be obtained at this time. However, he will be a frequent contributor and will lend the enterprise every encouragement possible. . . . Major J. K. Hudson will hold the position of editor-in-chief. The announcement that "Fighting Joe" will edit a Christian daily is causing much amusement here. Harold T. Chase will continue as associate editor. August Babize, of the *Times-Herald* of Chicago, who has bought stock in the *Capital,* will be news editor, having complete control of the news service. Mr. Popenoe says that the paper will advocate Republican principles, but will not say harsh things about political opponents, either in its own party or the opposition party. . . . Rev. Chas. W. Savidge, of Omaha, and Councilman C. C. Lobeck went to Topeka to interest Rev. Charles M. Sheldon in the work of the People's church at Omaha, of which Dr. Savidge is pastor. The church does work of a missionary character among the lower classes, and for that reason help was expected from Mr. Sheldon, but the visitors were disappointed. They were told there was no available space. Both men were very much disappointed, and Mr. Lobeck said: "I don't believe that Jesus would have turned us down after we had come 250 miles."

The Sheldon Edition of the *Capital*

The Topeka Daily Capital, March 20, 1900

The Topeka Daily Capital again assumes its sphere and work as a Republican daily newspaper. The experiment tried by Rev. Charles M. Sheldon from March 13 to March 18 in making a Christian daily is a matter of history. It has deeply interested millions of people. With the zealously religious people, at least with many of them, there is a sincere belief that the experiment will be a benefit in arousing interest in higher standards of journalism, while a large majority of people will refuse to see anything in it but the great zeal or an earnest evangelist in a strange field of labor.

The vast number of people who have read the Sheldon edition have been attracted to Mr. Sheldon's newspaper work because of his books, especially "In His Steps." The suggestion of Mr. Sheldon at the national meeting of the Endeavor society last year that some one give a million dollars to establish a Christian daily was the beginning of the experiment tried last week. One week was not long enough to test the idea, but it has aroused a discussion in every school district in the nation out of which much good will come to the readers as well as the publishers of newspapers, imperfect as the lesson of one week has been.

Running through the national comment, east and west, north and south, there is much harsh criticism. Mr. Sheldon is not spared, and as to this the Capital can only reiterate what it has heretofore said regarding the author of "In His Steps." No matter how widely one may differ from him regarding the experiment he has tried or the work he has done, all who come to know him recognize his intense earnestness, his unsullied integrity, his modesty and lack of all pretense. What he does is from a high conscientious sense of duty to which he addresses himself regardless of praise of [sic] criticism. Their [sic] is neither vanity or self-exaltation about the man, and the writer, who has seen Mr. Sheldon come and go here in Topeka in his work for years, can not but believe in his usefulness and that he is only upon the threshold of his life work.

The estimate placed upon Mr. Sheldon's experiment will generally be that it was a failure as a newspaper, and not above the average as a religious paper. The legitimate work of a newspaper is above all else to give the news. It may have a rich miscellany, a broad and intelligent editorial survey of the topics and issues of interest, but if it fails to give the general news from all parts of the world, as well as local and state news, without emasculation and censorship, it fails primarily in giving the people what they want, and have a right to have. The religious weeklies and monthlies of the country are edited by able men, and they offer in good form religious news and discussions of subjects appropriate for their columns that fully satisfy the general demand for special religious reading. On the other hand, the secular daily press in large cities is supported by unlimited capital and employs the ablest writers and best trained men for every department. Men equipped for news gathering and the treatment of any literary, scientific, military, educational or religious topic the world has ever seen. There are also a vast number of class papers covering every field of human labor in education, law, literature, science, reforms of all kinds, agriculture, trade and commerce in infinite variety. The daily and weekly newspapers fill fields entirely different and in no wise conflicting with illustrated weeklies, monthlies, critical reviews or class papers. The secular daily paper, whether partizan or independent, is not made for a class or a sect or a part of the people, but for all the people, and as such must offer its readers a paper free from sectarian religious bias.

Whether a daily paper is Republican, Democratic or Populist in politics it is made for all religious denominations, the Jew as well as the Methodist, the Catholic as well as the Presbyterian, and for the man who has no belief. That it should stand for all that builds a community, for all that makes good citizens, for clean municipal government, for honest political methods, for schools and churches and libraries, for the good name of the city, the state and the nation requires no argument. The press of the country today is on the side of law and order, it is against crime, it is for fairness and justice and as ready as any profession to champion the weak against the strong and to demand honesty and fair dealing.

The editor of the Capital has heretofore said in these columns that there is no field for the "Christian daily" and that there is no demand for such a publication. In the great centres of population with ample capital such a paper might be made self-sustaining in time, but it is gravely to be doubted. The Capital will in the future go forward upon the lines it has worked in the past as a Republican newspaper, improving all its departments from year to year, desirous of maintaining the confidence and good will of the people of Kansas for whom it labors.

12

Revivalism

The years following the Civil War saw rapid changes in transportation, communication, business and industry. The transcontinental railroad, the telegraph and finally the automobile bound the nation together, but also led to profound changes in the social fabric. With the means for acquiring raw materials and then shipping finished products throughout the country assured, manufacturing boomed, setting off a new wave of immigration and migration to the cities.

The changes affected even those who remained on farms or in the many small towns and villages. Mass production led to brand-name advertising. That, in turn, supported truly national mass media and led to market-driven local media. Increased dependence on commercial advertising for economic support produced changes in media content that made the comforts and culture of city life seem within easy reach of people everywhere.

While many embraced the changes, others greeted them with suspicion. Fear of the effects of city life and the new consumerism lay just below the surface as the Rev. Charles Sheldon started his "Jesus Newspaper." Although the end of the 19th century has never been labeled a third Great Awakening, it was an era of intense religious activity. Protestant churches and itinerant clergy renewed their efforts to weld the newly reunited states into a Protestant Christian nation. As in the Second Great Awakening, evangelistic campaigns and revivals kept many within the Protestant mainstream. But the religious fervor also paved the way for new responses, both within Protestantism and outside its fold.

In spite of the Rev. Sheldon's concern that newspapers were not giving proper attention to religion, stories of church activities and support for their revivals and other causes were staples of news coverage. *McClure's Magazine* routinely published Bible commentaries, accounts of trips to the Holy Land and other articles contributed by clergy authors; *Godey's Ladies Book* carried articles designed to help women create a Christian home.

However, as newspapers came to rely less on contributors and more on their own professional reporters, news style changed. The "First State

Convention of the Y.M.C.A. of Ohio" tells of the efforts within one state to revitalize one of the most influential of the 19th-century organizations for ministering to the needs of those who moved to the cities. As was common for the period, the story unfolds in chronological order, giving to it the character of minutes of a meeting. "Moody's Start" is a later example of the use of a story that was picked up from another paper. In contrast to that story, told in the first person by the noted evangelist, "Aged Missionary's Tour" illustrates the new emphasis on colorful writing and narrative; "Billy Sunday on the Rampage at Columbus, Ohio" mixes the inverted pyramid form with the journalist's commentary. "A New Mission," about the first worship service held by Nazarenes in Los Angeles, illustrates the emerging news style with its emphasis on precise names, facts and figures as well as the developing trend toward using staff reporters to cover Sunday worship services and other meetings of religious organizations that was typical from about 1880, when church pages were introduced, until the mid-1900s.

While popular evangelists such as Dwight Moody and Billy Sunday became national figures and media darlings at the turn of the century, their old-style revivalism appealed more to the middle class than to others. On March 18, 1897, the *Ohio State Journal* published a story documenting early efforts to organize and promote a turn-of-the-century kind of New Age spirituality. In "Weird Babel of Tongues" reproduced in this chapter, choice of language and detail provide a vivid word picture of the birth of Pentecostalism, but the same choices that make the story so compelling also illustrate the tendency of outside observers to impose mainstream judgments on unconventional religions.

First State Convention of the Y.M.C.A. of Ohio

The Morning Journal, November 9, 1867

Columbus, Friday, October 8

A number of delegates to the Convention being in the city, a meeting was called at 11 o'clock A.M., at the Congregational Church, for devotional exercises, preparatory to entering upon the regular business of the Convention this afternoon—H. Thane Miller, of Cincinnati, in the chair. The meeting was opened by singing, after which Hon. C. N. Olds read a Scripture lesson from the 2d chapter of the 1st Epistle of John, beginning at the 7th and ending with the 17th verse. An hour was spent in in [sic] singing and prayer and remarks by various members of the Convention.

2½ O'CLOCK, P.M.

The Convention met according to previous arrangement, and was called to order by H. W. Cheever, of Cincinnati, and joined in singing, "Ask and ye shall receive," after which prayer was offered by Rev. G. S. Chase, of this city.

Hon. C. N. Olds, of Columbus, was elected temporary chairman.

Mr. Olds, on taking the chair, stated that in obedience to resolutions passed by the Convention of the Young Men's Christian Associations of the United States and British Provinces, held in Montreal in June last, State Conventions had been called in various States of the Union and were yet to be called in others. In obedience to a call by delegates to that Convention, from this State, this Convention meets to-day.

Bro. H. J. Rowland of Cincinnati was then elected temporary Secretary.

On motion of H. J. Sheldon, of Toledo, a committee of five were appointed to nominate permanent officers to consist of a President, four Vice Presidents and two Recording Secretaries. The following Committee was appointed by the Chair:

H. J. Sheldon, of Toledo; Samuel Chester, of Cincinnati; Woodward Awl, of Columbus; J. J. Wilson, of Cleveland; M. M. Saunders, of Painesville.

During the absence of this Committee, the Convention spent a few moments in devotional exercises.

The Committee on Permanent Organization then made the following report:

For President—H. Thane Miller, of Cincinnati.

For Vice Presidents—Rev. A. J. Lyon, of Sandusky; Rev. P. C. Prugh, Xenia; Rev. W. C. Tisdale, Painesville; C. E. Bolton, Cleveland.

For Secretaries—R. S. Fulton, Cincinnati; H. A. Sherman, Cleveland.

On motion, the report was adopted.

ADDRESS OF WELCOME.

Upon the President elect taking the chair, Capt. Wm. Mitchell, of Columbus, made, on behalf of the Young Men's Christian Association of Columbus, the following address of welcome to the delegates from abroad:

MR. PRESIDENT AND BRETHREN: It becomes my pleasant duty, this afternoon, on behalf of the Young Men's Christian Association of this city—and I believe I may speak on behalf of the Christian community in general, and not only of them but of all well-wishers of the public good—in behalf of these brethren of the Association, and our christian brethren in the city in general, and on behalf of all good citizens of our city, I bid you a welcome among us. We come together as fellow workers in the vineyard of the Lord. The field is a large one and the harvest is an immense one, but we may say as one said of old truly, "the laborers are few." We have our churches, the light of the world, a city set on its hill, but it appears as though in this Young Men's Christian Association there is something akin to that plan sometimes adopted by military forces when the strongholds of the enemy are to be taken, and it is necessary often to penetrate within their lines. They sometimes organize a "forlorn hope" composed of soldiers from different regiments and battallions and corps to force the enemy from his works, so from the different churches we have organized our forces for a special work, and I believe it is our duty often to penetrate within the lines of the ememy and to lay our plans of attack upon the enemy. The work truly is a great one. We hope, as residents of this city, for much good from your coming among us. We have here a great field, and a great work to do; but we feel like going forward and doing all we can to accomplish this great work. We hope we will be greatly strengthened and helped in this glorious work by your coming among us. We hope that your coming up from different parts of the State, with zeal in your hearts, and with your good counsels while among us, will kindle such a fire in our hearts as shall greatly interest us, and that our young men, in the light of this fire, will be induced to lead lives of holiness, happiness and usefulness.

I bid you into our midst, to our homes, and to our hearts, a heartfelt and earnest welcome.

REPLY OF THE PRESIDENT, H. THANE MILLER OF CINCINNATI.

Brethren of the first State Convention of the Young Men's Christian Association of Ohio:

I need not assure you that I consider it a very great honor that has been conferred upon me in electing me President of a Convention like